That's Here?

25 Historical Places to Visit

In & Around

Sheridan, Wyoming

Copyright Page

Cover image: Fort Phil Kearny

Back cover image: Historic Sheridan Inn

Photos and maps provided by author.

Please note when using maps: Maps are not to scale. Interstate 90 runs north and south through Northeast, Wyoming and Southern Montana, but it is still referred to on maps as I-90 east and west.

Information such as dates of upcoming events and prices for entry are all subject to change. Please contact individual sites for the latest prices and confirmed dates.

Copyright © David Wooten. 2012
   All Rights Reserved

Contents

1. Sheridan, Wyoming 8
2. Sheridan Inn 12
3. Mandel Cabin 16
4. Kendrick Mansion 20
5. Fort Mackenzie 24
6. Crook's Camp 28
7. Rosebud Camp 32
8. Skirmish at Tongue River Heights 36
9. Fort Phil Kearny 40
10. Fetterman Battlefield 44
11. Wagon Box Fight 48
12. Bozeman Trail 52
13. Connor Battlefield 56
14. Sawyer Fight 60
15. Tongue River 64
16. Buffalo, Wyoming 70
17. Occidental Hotel 74
18. Big Horn, Wyoming 80
19. Bradford Brinton Memorial 84
20. Dayton, Wyoming 88
21. Little Bighorn Battlefield 94
22. Devil's Tower 98
23. Pompey's Pillar 102
24. Medicine Wheel 106
25. Deer Medicine Rocks 110

Contents Cont.

Historic Downtown Sheridan 113
More to See 119
Sheridan Area Museums 123
Sheridan Area Historic Events 126

For Candice:

Who was with me every step of the way. I could not have done this without you.

Sheridan Area

1

~SHERIDAN, WYOMING~

HISTORY: In 1882, pioneer John Loucks came to Wyoming from Montana and plotted the town of Sheridan on the back of some brown wrapping paper. Only a few years before, this area along the Bighorn Mountains had been a part of the Plains Indians hunting grounds. The "Bloody" Bozeman Trail cut through it on its way to the gold fields of Montana, and it was the location that Oglala Sioux war chief Crazy Horse talked of having his own reservation. It was a wild and dangerous land then, but soon after the arrival of John Loucks it would become a small city with all the conveniences of modern society.

Loucks chose the town's name as a tribute to his Civil War General, Philip Sheridan. He started Sheridan's first bank, general store, and post office all from inside his small cabin. He would be

Sheridan's first mayor, and one of Sheridan's main streets still bears his name.

When the railroad arrived in 1892 the town boomed, attracting the likes of Buffalo Bill Cody and Calamity Jane. Buffalo Bill ran the Sheridan Inn for many years, using it as the western base of operations for his Wild West Show.

The advent of the railroad brought cattleman, and soon there were ranches where the buffalo once roamed. Sheridan, while still relatively small, was on its way to becoming one of the largest towns in Wyoming. By 1910 over 10,000 people called Sheridan home.

Scottish brothers William and Malcolm Moncrieffe introduced polo to the area in the late 1800's, building some of the first polo fields west of the Mississippi River. Now, over 120 years later, the Sheridan area plays host to world class polo with international players from across the globe.

In 1931, the annual Sheridan WYO Rodeo began. Rodeo fans from all over the world converge on Sheridan each July to enjoy 4 days of professional rodeo action.

Today, Sheridan is a tourist haven with great hunting and fishing accessible in the nearby Bighorn Mountains. Golfers can tee it up at the Powder Horn, voted one of the *Best Residential Courses in the United Sates*, and history enthusiasts descend on Sheridan for its proximity to The Little Bighorn Battlefield and other historic Indian War sites like Fort Phil Kearny, the Wagon Box and Rosebud Battlefields.

Downtown Sheridan's rich history is still very much alive, as 30 buildings on the *National Register of Historical Places* are still in use. Visitors can have a beer in the 100 year old Mint Bar, then cross the street to visit King's Saddlery Museum home to Western memorabilia from all over the United States, including saddles belonging to Gene Autry and pants worn by John Wayne in one of his westerns.

In 2006, Sheridan was named the *#1 Western Town in America* by True West magazine, and in 2012, Western Horseman magazine named Sheridan the *King of Cowboy Towns*.

WHAT'S THERE TODAY: Most of the historic buildings in downtown Sheridan are still in use. The area where General George Crook and his soldiers camped after being defeated at the Battle of the Rosebud is just off of downtown, as is John Louck's original cabin where Sheridan's history began.

You can enjoy dinner at the famous Sheridan Inn, where Buffalo Bill Cody set up residence, or tour the Kendrick Mansion, home to one-time Wyoming Governor and U.S. Senator John B. Kendrick. Sheridan is also in close proximity to many Indian War historic sites, including the Battle of the Little Bighorn where George Armstrong Custer died, the Rosebud Battlefield, and Fort Phil Kearny.

ADDITIONAL INFORMATION: The Sheridan County Museum on 5th Street is full of information about the area's history, as is the Wyoming Information Center off of 5th Street (next to Interstate 90 at Exit 23). For more info call 307.673.7120.

WEBSITES: www.sheridanwyoming.org
www.sheridanhistoricalsociety.com
www.visitsheridanwyoming.com

SHERIDAN COUNTY COURTHOUSE

DIRECTIONS

Sheridan, Wyoming, is 130 miles south of Billings, Montana, and nearly the same distance north of Casper, Wyoming, on Interstate 90.

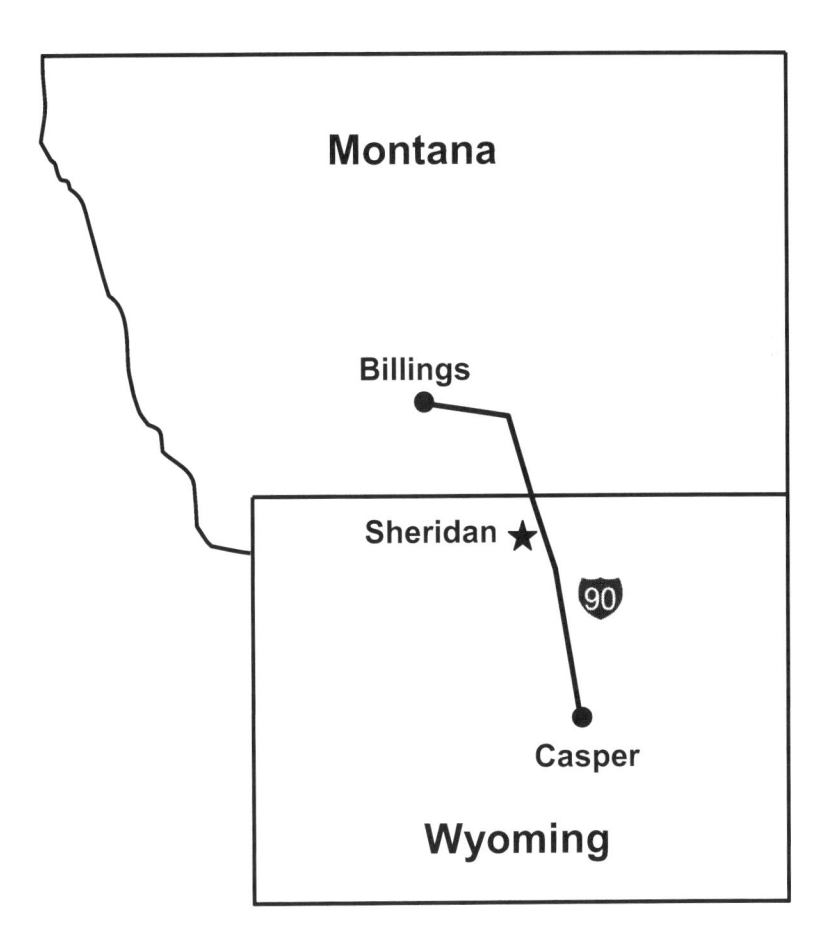

2

~Sheridan Inn~

History: Buffalo Bill Cody set up shop here and Ernest Hemingway is said to have written a part of *A Farewell to Arms* while staying as a guest. Some also believe it to be haunted. The Sheridan Inn has enjoyed a rich and exciting history since it was opened on May 27th, 1893.

It was built by the Burlington and Missouri Railroad in partnership with the Sheridan Land Company, and at the time was considered to be one of the finest hotels between Chicago and San Francisco. Buffalo Bill Cody ran the inn—although he never owned it—from 1894 to 1901. Cody used the Inn as a western headquarters for his Wild West Show. Behind the Inn, Buffalo Bill built stables and barns. From here he operated the W.F. Cody Transportation Company, the stagecoach that ran between Sheridan and Deadwood, South Dakota.

In its early days $2.25 could get you a room, and a meal was only 50 cents. It was the first building in Sheridan wired for electricity, and it had a phone connected to a downtown drugstore.

Throughout the late 1800's and early 1900's, the Sheridan Inn was the social center of Sheridan. It is said that men on horseback would sometimes ride their mounts up to the bar, while lavish parties were thrown in its huge dining hall. The Sheridan Inn was a meeting place for the famous and wealthy.

In 1964 the Sheridan Inn was placed on the National Register of Historic Places.

Soon after, though, the Inn fell in disrepair and was condemned. It was eventually bought up by a developer who had plans to demolish it. Wanting to preserve one of Sheridan's pillars, the Sheridan Historical Society sponsored a "Save the Inn" campaign, eventually finding a new owner who reopened it two years later.

Today the Sheridan Inn remains a vestige of the town's earlier days. A time when the West was still wild, and America was on its way to becoming a worldwide power.

SHERIDAN INN VERANDA

WHAT'S THERE TODAY: Outside you can take a walk on the wide veranda where Buffalo Bill used to sit as he auditioned acts for his Wild West Show, while inside you can still enjoy a drink at the famous Buffalo Bill Bar.

In the lobby is the original hotel registration desk with a copy of the hotel registry from 1893, showing Buffalo Bill Cody's signature. There is also an original fireplace in the lobby with black and white photographs along the walls highlighting the hotel's early days. And in the dining room you can walk below large spans of Georgia pine that witnessed many a dance with Buffalo Bill serving as host.

Upstairs rooms are currently being renovated, and you'll eventually be able to stay the night where Ernest Hemingway, President Herbert Hoover, Will Rogers, and Bob Hope once slept. And if you're lucky, perhaps you'll catch a glimpse of Miss Kate, who is believed to still roam the historic building.

Catherine B. Arnold, known as Miss Kate, worked at the Inn for 64 years as a seamstress, desk clerk, housekeeper, hostess, and babysitter. In 1968, when Miss Kate passed away, her ashes were buried in one of the 3rd floor walls. Employees of the Sheridan Inn and guests have reported lights turning on and off, and doors opening and shutting on their own, a phenomenon they believe is linked to Miss Kate.

> **ADDITIONAL INFORMATION:** There is a restaurant residing inside the Inn that offers lunch and dinner. The Sheridan Inn is just blocks away from Historic Downtown Sheridan with shopping, restaurants, and other historic buildings.
>
> Tours of the Inn are sometimes available. To check on tour availability and other information about the Sheridan Inn call 307-674-2178.

WEBSITE: www.sheridaninn.com

DIRECTIONS

From Interstate 90 in Sheridan, take Exit #23 (5th Street). The Inn is 1 mile west on 5th Street, just over the railroad tracks.

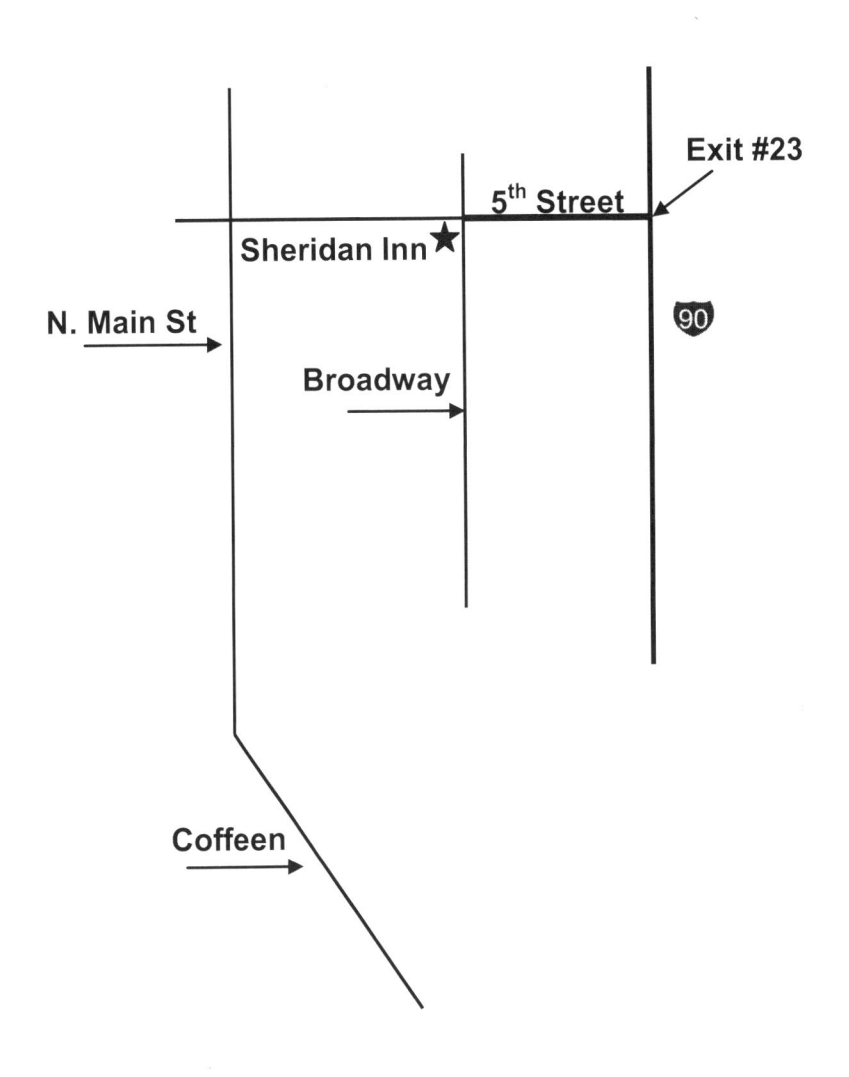

3

~Mandel Cabin~

History: Trapper "Dutch Henry" built the Mandel Cabin near the confluence of Big and Little Goose Creeks in 1878. Only two years before, General George Crook camped here, using the spot as a staging area for his assault against Crazy Horse and Sitting Bull. The Mandel Cabin would be the first structure in what would eventually become the town of Sheridan, Wyoming.

Henry abandoned his cabin the next year and George Mandel took it over, establishing a post office and setting himself up as postmaster. In 1882, John D. Loucks bought the dirt floored, sod roof cabin, adding some shelves and a counter and opening up a store. He used a bed sheet to separate the store from his living quarters. It was here that Loucks plotted the town of Sheridan on the back of some brown wrapping paper.

The Mandel Cabin served as Sheridan's first post office, general store, church, schoolhouse, and was the site of the area's first territorial election. It was also used as a lawyer's office and library.

At some point a second story was added, and in 1885, E.A. Whitney purchased the cabin, living in its upstairs living quarters. Whitney moved the cabin to the corner of Loucks & Main where it became part of the town's first bank, the Bank of Sheridan. The park where the Mandel Cabin now resides is named after Whitney, who made the cabin his home until his death in 1917.

Over the years the cabin was moved several times, becoming part of another building at one point, and eventually falling into disrepair. In 1976-77, The National Society of Colonial Dames of America in the state of Wyoming hired out to restore the cabin to its original one-room structure that you can see today.

> When I got to the brow of the hill where the court house now stands overlooking the Big Goose valley, I was tired and hungry so sat down to rest for awhile. It was a beautiful spring evening and the sun was just going down over the Big Horn Mountains. The grass was beginning to show green and over across Little Goose was a herd of buffalo coming down into the valley to water. Up Big Goose a small herd of deer was browsing, and it all appealed to me as an ideal site for our city. . .I arose and slowly walked to my lonely cabin, built a fire, cooked my supper, ate it and with the aid of a candle, took a sheet of brown wrapping paper, marked off forty acres, and laid out a town with the streets all named after the few settlers. Over the top of the map I wrote "Sheridan" in big letters.
>
> John D. Loucks
> Founder of Sheridan

WHAT'S THERE TODAY: The Mandel Cabin is tucked away in the Dorothy King Reflective Garden in Whitney Commons Park. It is within sight of where the cabin was initially built back in 1878.

Most of the logs are from the original structure. The roof, floor, door, and window frames have been reconstructed with lumber from an earlier extension.

The cabin is decorated with furnishings of the era, some of which are from old Fort Custer in Montana.

> **ADDITIONAL INFORMATION:** The cabin is accessible 7 days a week. Whitney Commons Park offers pedestrian walks, kid's playground, and restroom facilities.
>
> The cabin is owned and maintained by The National Society of The Colonial Dames of America in the State of Wyoming.
>
> For information about tours of the cabin call **307.675.1150**.

WEBSITE: www.sheridanwyoming.org

FOUNTAIN IN DOROTHY KING REFLECTIVE GARDEN

DIRECTIONS

The Mandel Cabin is located one block west of Historic Downtown Sheridan near the corner of Brooks & Alger. The cabin is across from the Sheridan County Fulmer Library in Whitney Commons Park.

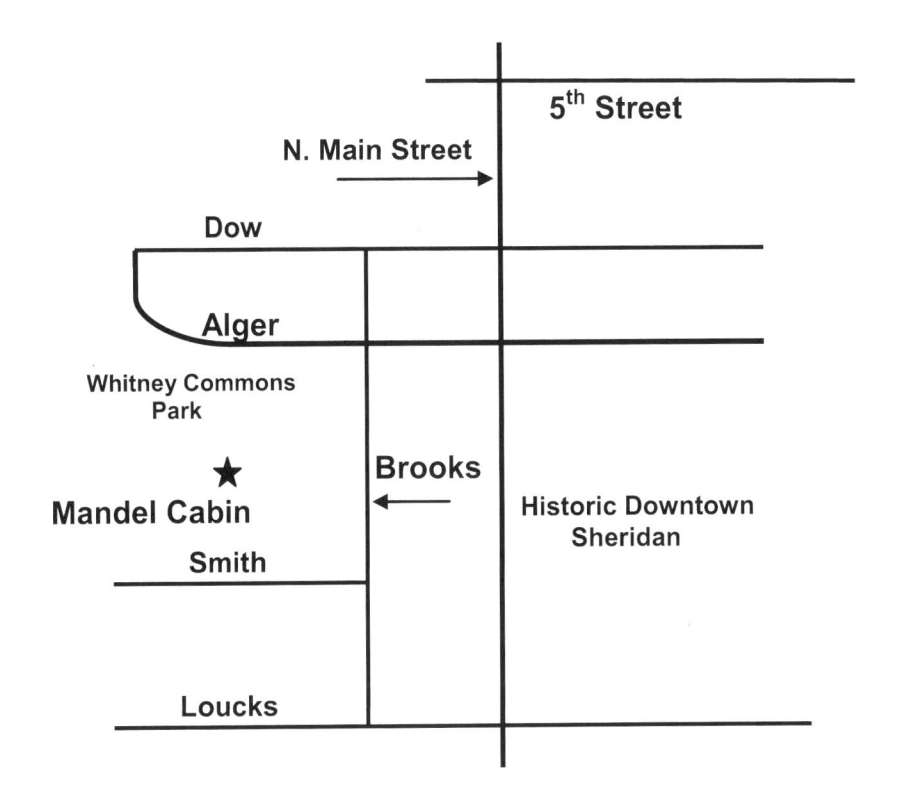

4

~Kendrick Mansion~

History: The Kendrick Mansion is the former home of the once governor of Wyoming and 3-time U.S. Senator, John B. Kendrick.

Kendrick, orphaned at a young age, came to Wyoming from Texas as a poor trail hand on a cattle drive. With very little formal education, John B. Kendrick managed to build up a small cattle empire (he owned over 200,000 acres in southern Montana and northern Wyoming) that he used to launch a successful political career.

He served in the Wyoming Senate from 1910 to 1914 (while the mansion was being built) and then was elected governor, where he served from 1915-17. He resigned to become a U.S. Senator, where he was reelected twice (1922, 1928), serving from 1917 until his death in 1933.

Kendrick commenced building on the mansion in 1908, finishing in 1913 at a cost of $165,000 (nearly $4 million dollars in today's money). Kendrick would refer to his new home as Trail End; a symbolic reference to his cattle trail days. Designed by Montana architect Glen Charles McAlister, the mansion is a mix of styles. American Gothic, late Victorian, Edwardian, and Prairie enhance the interior, while Flemish revival and Neoclassical make up the bulk of the exterior. It sits atop a hill overlooking all of Sheridan to the east, while a majestic view of the Bighorn Mountains can be taken in to the south and west. In Kendrick's day there were lovely rose gardens, and even a grass tennis court adorning the grounds.

The mansion that took five years to build would only serve as the main family residence for a short time. Late in 1914 Kendrick was elected Governor of Wyoming, sending the family to Cheyenne. Two years later the family would move to Washington D.C., upon his election to the United States Senate. The family would return to Trail End for summer recesses, but the mansion would never again serve as their full-time residence.

After Kendrick's death in 1933, various family members moved in and out of the residence for several years. By the early 60's the mansion stood empty. Attempts were made to sell the mansion but none were successful. The "Castle on the Hill," as many Sheridan residents referred to it, was close to being demolished for new condominiums.

Thanks to donated money from private individuals and state agencies, the Sheridan Historical Society was able to purchase the land, while Kendrick heirs donated the mansion and its contents.

Mounting costs to run the mansion eventually led the Sheridan County Historical Society to turn Trail End over to the State of Wyoming, which runs the mansion today.

Trail End was placed on the National Register of Historic Places in 1970.

KENDRICK MANSION FROM DRIVEWAY

WHAT'S THERE TODAY: A tour of the 13,000 square foot mansion is like taking a trip back in time to the early part of the twentieth century.

There is an upstairs grand ballroom, library, maid's quarters and a guest wing. You can visit John Kendrick's old bedroom, and see where the family gathered for their meals.

Behind the mansion on the west side is the 3,013 square foot Carriage House. Once used as a small apartment for Kendrick while his mansion was being built, it later housed his riding horses and automobiles. Today the Carriage House is an 88-seat community theater.

ADDITIONAL INFORMATION: The Kendrick Mansion is open daily from March to December. Site grounds are open year round until sunset. Tours are sometimes available. There is a small entrance fee. 307.674.4589.

WEBSITE: www.trailend.org

Directions

Take the 5th Street exit off Interstate 90 (Exit 23). Proceed west towards Sheridan on 5th Street. Go past Main Street and turn left on Clarendon. Continue on Clarendon for six blocks. The mansion will be visible where the street dead ends. Parking is available on surrounding streets. Handicapped parking is provided.

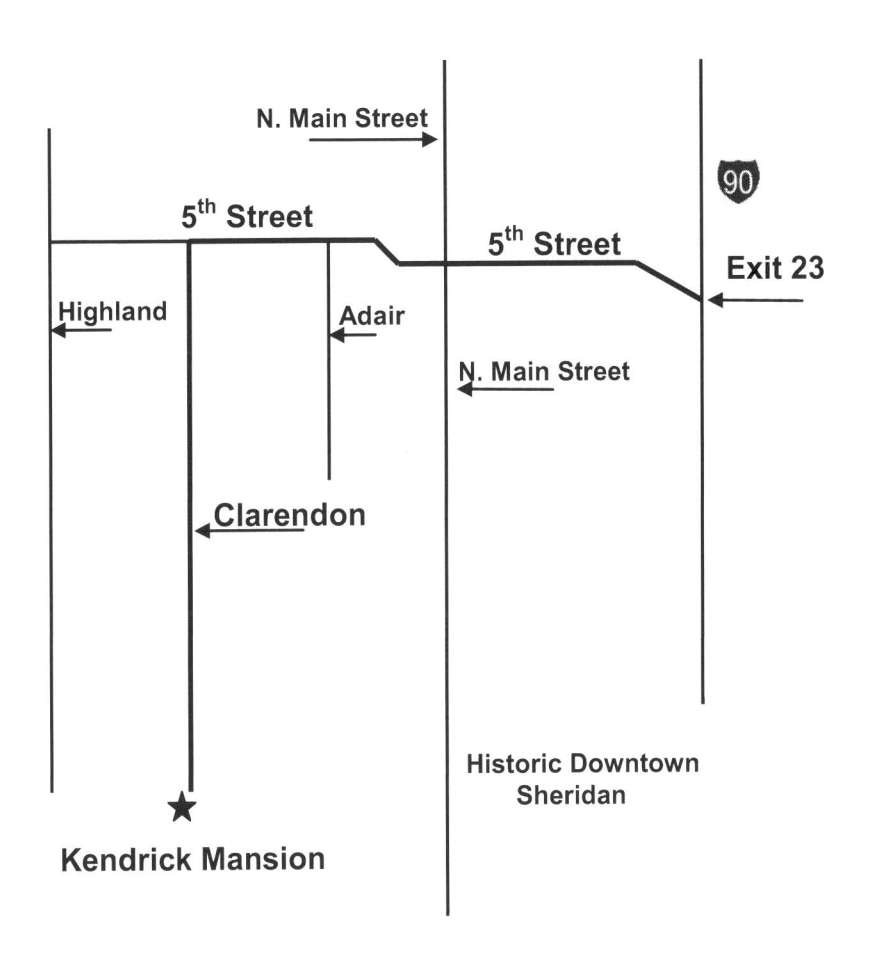

5

~Fort Mackenzie~

History: The first temporary structures at Fort Mackenzie went up in 1899. What had been the heart of Indian Territory a quarter of a century before was now quiet prairie, but several local businessmen decided that if they could get the military to build a post in Sheridan it would greatly improve the local economy. A delegation of prominent citizens was promptly dispatched to Washington, and a year later the government broke ground on Fort Mackenzie.

The fort is named for Brigadier General Ranald Mackenzie, who rose in ranks during the Civil War and the Indian Wars. It was home to the 2nd and 3rd Battalions of the 18th Infantry in 1901, and in 1902 the Buffalo Soldiers recuperated there after fighting in Cuba and the Philippines.

The fort came close to being demolished just before World War II, but former President Taft intervened, getting the fort transferred to the Bureau of Health. It became a hospital with 300 beds for injured soldiers returning home from World War I. By the end of World War II it was a 900 bed facility. In 1972 it was placed on the National Register of Historic Places.

Today Fort Mackenzie is a V.A. Hospital with over 200 beds, serving 12,000 veterans annually.

WHAT'S THERE TODAY: Some of the buildings date back to the early 1900's, and are still in use today. The grounds have a terrific view of the Bighorn Mountains, along with a Frisbee golf course.

> **ADDITIONAL INFORMATION:** The Sheridan VA Hospital is now situated on approximately 272 acres of land, down from the 6,280 acres that once made up the Fort Mackenzie complex. Over one-half of the buildings today within the hospital grounds were constructed in the first decade of the twentieth century when Fort Mackenzie was a military post. For more info call **307.672.3473**.

WEBSITE: www.sheridan.va.gov

ENTRANCE TO FORT MACKENZIE

DIRECTIONS

Exit 20 off of I-90. Go south on North Main Street. Turn right on Fort Road. From downtown Sheridan take North Main Street and turn left on Fort Road.

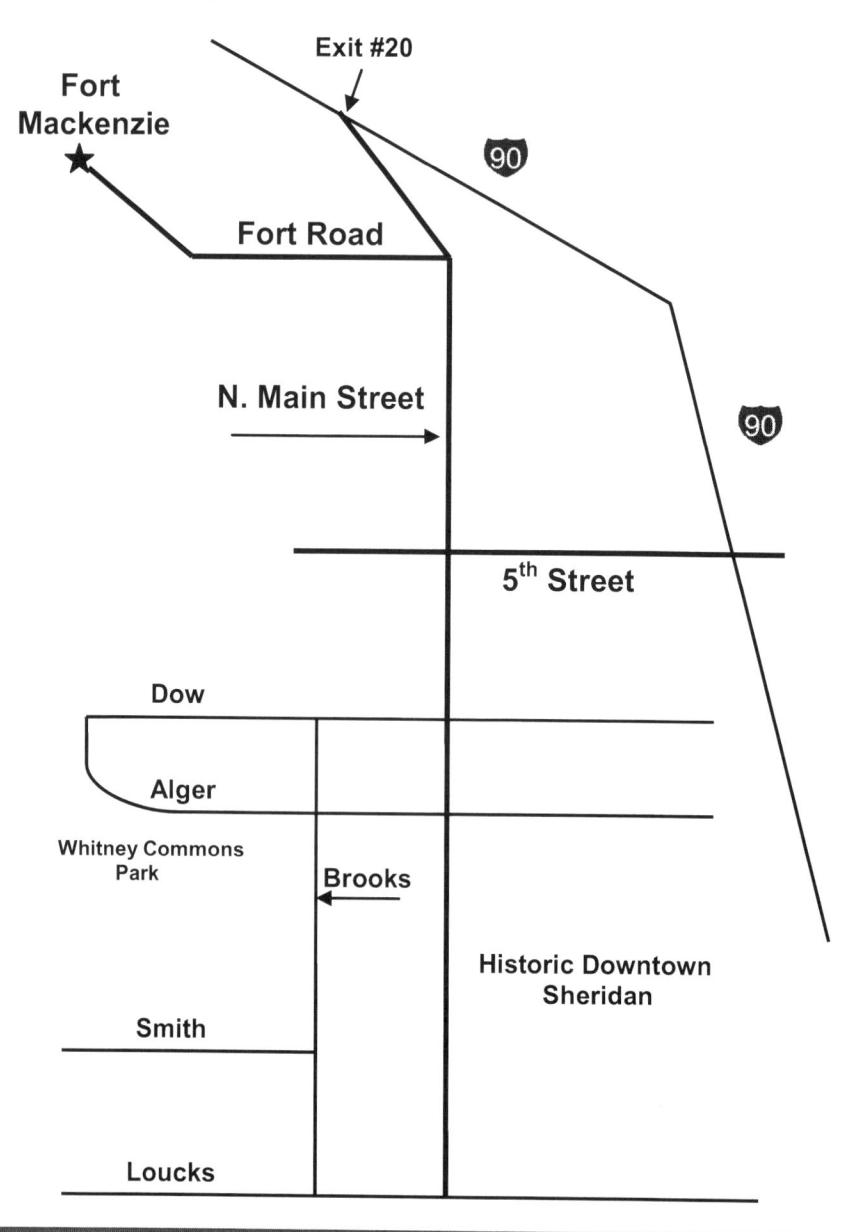

Indian Wars

6

~Crook's Camp~

HISTORY: When George Armstrong Custer and his 7th Cavalry lost their lives at the Battle of the Little Bighorn, General George Crook was camped with nearly 1300 soldiers in and around what is now present day Sheridan, Wyoming. Had Crook's column been 70 miles north—where they had planned to be—history may have been changed.

Crook's regiment was part of a three-pronged attack that the Army hoped would hem in the renegade Indian warriors they were after, led by Crazy Horse and Sitting Bull.

Marching his division up from Fort Fetterman (near Douglas, Wyoming), Crook's plan was to meet up with Colonel John Gibbons company moving down from Fort Ellis (Bozeman, Montana), and

General Alfred H. Terry with Custer's 7th Cavalry, marching in from Fort Abraham Lincoln (Bismarck, North Dakota).

Crook made his base camp at the confluence of Little and Big Goose Creeks (present day Sheridan, Wyoming), and waited for his Crow and Shoshone scouts to arrive. He then left behind his wagons and ambulances—he didn't want them to slow him down—and proceeded up into Montana to Rosebud Creek. Each man was allowed to carry 1 blanket, 100 rounds of ammunition, and four day's rations. The infantry were mounted on mules.

On June 17, 1876, (8 days before the Battle of the Little Bighorn) Crook's force would be the first to encounter the Indians the Army was hoping to find. At what is now known as the Battle of the Rosebud, Crook and his men fought over 1000 warriors led by Crazy Horse. The fight lasted 6 hours, and Crook suffered 10 dead and over 20 wounded. Exhausting most of his ammunition, Crook withdrew back to his base along Little and Big Goose Creeks.

Despite the fact that Crook called the fight a victory, his command was for all practical purposes knocked out of the Army's Powder River Campaign.

Crook and his beleaguered troops spent seven weeks camped along Big Goose Creek in the Sheridan area, holding fishing competitions with each other to pass their idle time. Lt. John Bourke reported in his notebook that hundreds of cutthroat trout were caught by the men in one day.

It wasn't until August, when reinforcements arrived, that Crook and his men started back out again to reunite with Terry's army and what was left of Custer's command. Buffalo Bill Cody had joined the expedition by this time, boasting he was going to claim the "first scalp for Custer!"

Had Crook's column defeated Crazy Horse and his warriors at the Battle of the Rosebud, and not been forced to retreat back to the Sheridan area, the Battle of the Little Bighorn may have had a different outcome for Custer and his 7th Cavalry.

CLOUD PEAK BOULDER

WHAT'S THERE TODAY: The site of Crook's camp in Sheridan is marked by an historic sign and rock fountain. The confluence of Little Goose Creek and Big Goose Creek has changed since Crook's time, but visitors are still surrounded by the hills and bluffs where Crook's soldiers made their camp.

And while the course of Big Goose Creek has been altered in the area of downtown Sheridan, it still follows most of its original course through nearby Kendrick Park where some of Crook's command would have been camped.

> **ADDITIONAL INFORMATION:** From present day Sheridan, Crook moved his men higher up along Little Goose Creek, closer to the Bighorn Mountains. In 1954, a large stone (see picture above) was unearthed near Little Goose Canyon where Crook's men made their final camp. The names of two of Crook's scouts (Grouard and Pourior) are carved on it, along with the date: June 23, 1876 (2 days before the Battle of the Little Bighorn). The stone is on display at the Bozeman Trail Museum (see page 124), in Big Horn Wyoming.

WEBSITE: www.sheridanwyoming.org

DIRECTIONS

Crook's campsite is a block off Main Street, near the corner of Dow and Lewis streets. From Interstate 90 take the 5th St exit (Exit 23) and go west into Sheridan. Turn left onto Main St from 5th. Turn right at the first light (Dow Street) and the monument is one block on the left side.

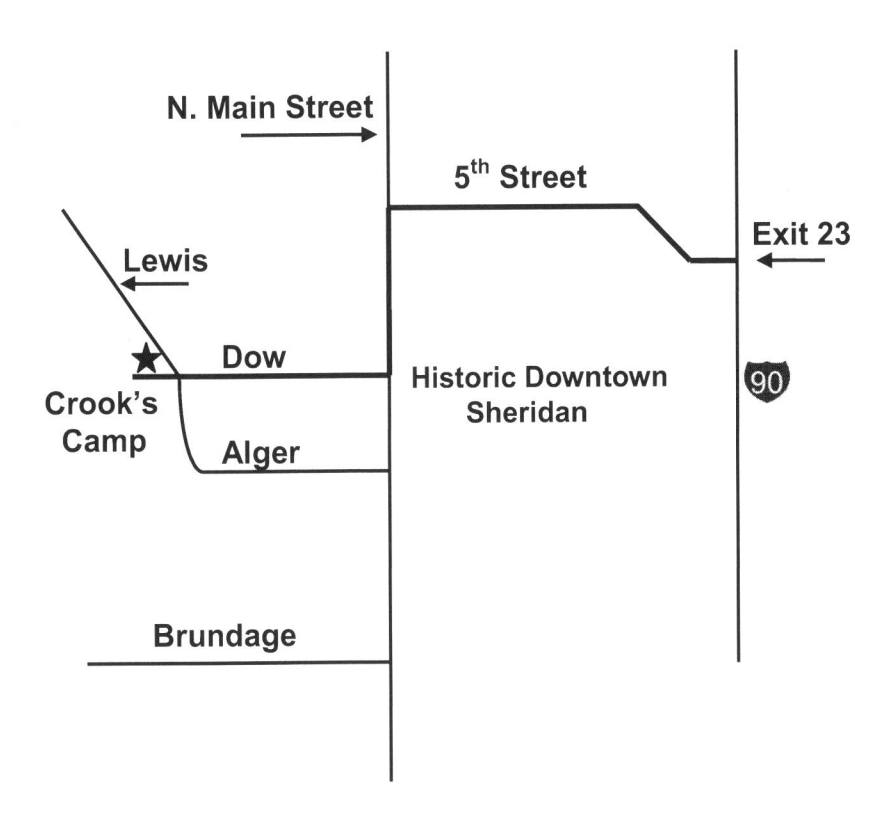

7

~Rosebud Battlefield~

History: On June 17, 1876, eight days before the Battle of the Little Bighorn, many of the same warriors that defeated George Armstrong Custer met the U.S. Army on a small tributary in southeastern Montana known as Rosebud Creek. To whites the fight is known as The Battle of the Rosebud, while the Cheyenne Indians call it The Battle Where the Girl Saved her Brother. So named from an incident in the fight, when a Cheyenne warrior's horse was shot out from under him and his sister rode in to rescue him.

The fight drew one of the largest contingents of Indians ever assembled to do battle with the U.S. Army—until the Battle of the Little Bighorn a week later. Nearly one thousand Indian warriors rode all night from their main camp on Ash Creek to meet General George Crook and his soldiers that day on the Rosebud.

Outside of historians and army buffs, very few people have studied this battle that in many ways helped shape the Battle of the Little Bighorn. Crook's troops were on the Rosebud that day looking for a large contingent of renegade Indians led by Sitting Bull and Crazy Horse. The Indians had been ordered onto the Reservation; but when they refused to come in, the Army moved out to force the issue. Crook's column was pushing northward to meet up with Custer's troops coming down from the Yellowstone River. Crook's column had left Big Goose Creek (present day Sheridan, Wyoming) the day before. They had marched some forty miles and after breaking camp very early on the morning of the 17th, had stopped to rest and have coffee along the Rosebud about 8am.

Around 8:30am the soldiers were attacked, alerted by their Crow and Shoshone scouts who were racing back to camp just ahead of their Sioux and Cheyenne pursuers.

The fight lasted for six hours, the fronts changing from hilltop to hilltop into early afternoon. Dust and gunpowder hung thick in the air as Indians and soldiers fought for the slightest advantage. At one point, Crook dispatched Captain Anson Mills to take some cavalry to find the main village of Indians; he believed to be in the area. Unbeknownst to Crook, the village was nearly 40 miles away, and when the Sioux and Cheyenne intensified their fight, he quickly sent a messenger to bring Mills back. When Mills returned the Indians decided to call it a day. Crook's men had suffered 10 dead and 21 wounded. Indian losses were about the same.

Crook was forced to retreat back to Goose Creek, and although he called the battle a victory, the fight effectively knocked him out of the campaign. It is left to speculation as to what would have happened at the Battle of the Little Bighorn had Crook's 1000 plus soldiers been there to assist Custer.

> "Looking behind I saw a dozen Sioux surrounding a group of soldiers who had straggled behind the retreat. Six were killed at one spot."
>
> Reuben Briggs Davenport
> Reporter, New York Herald

ROSEBUD BATTLEFIELD

WHAT'S THERE TODAY: The battlefield remains pretty much the same as it did the day of the battle back in 1876. You can stand atop the same hilltop where General Crook set up his field headquarters to command the battle, and view the area along the Rosebud where Crook's troops were camped when the battle began. There is also a buffalo jump dating back to 3,000 B.C., ancient tipi rings, eagle catching pits, and rock cairns.

ADDITIONAL INFORMATION: The Rosebud Battlefield wasn't established as a state park until 1978. While there are plans to upgrade the park, the site is still rather primitive. There is no visitor's center, only a bathroom and a few interpretive markers.

Northern Cheyenne view the Rosebud as sacred ground and hold ceremonies at the site honoring the warriors and the soldiers who fought and died there.

Be aware that during hunting season the park is open for antelope, deer, and upland game bird hunting. Rattlesnakes can be abundant in the summer months, so be cautious.

For more information about the site you can contact Rosebud Battlefield State park at **406.757.2219**.

WEBSITE:
http://stateparks.mt.gov/parks/visit/rosebudBattlefield/

Directions

Take Decker Road (Hwy 338) north from Sheridan about 45 miles and follow the signs. Note: **Wyoming Hwy 338 turns into Montana Hwy 314 at the Wyoming/Montana state border.**

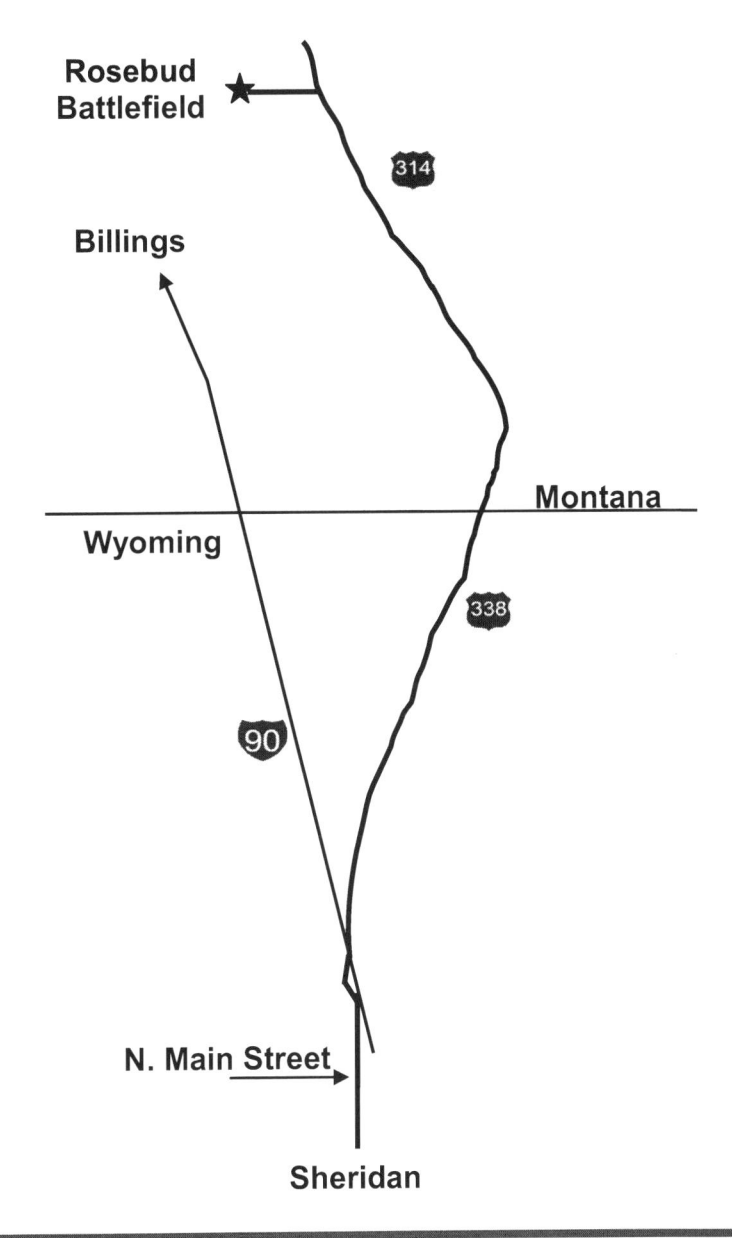

8

~Skirmish at Tongue River Heights~

History: 10 days before the Battle of the Rosebud and just over two weeks prior to the Battle of the Little Bighorn, General George Crook and his command of a thousand soldiers made camp next to the Tongue River, just west of where it intersects with Prairie Dog Creek.

Two days later on June 9, 1876, Sioux and Cheyenne Indians made a show of force on the bluffs across from their camp on the Tongue River. The Indians were too far away to do much damage with their breech loading rifles, but they did manage to fray some nerves in Crook's camp.

Crook dispatched a battalion of men led by Captain Anson Mills, who crossed the Tongue and drove the Indians from off the bluff.

Two Indians were reportedly killed. The army lost 3 horses and one mule.

Crook broke camp two days later, moving back to present day Sheridan, Wyoming, along Goose Creek. 8 days later Crook and his men would battle again with these same Indians—along with nearly 800 other warriors—at the Battle of the Rosebud.

Below is a newspaper account of the skirmish written in the New York Herald on June 16, 1876, by Reuben Briggs Davenport, a reporter traveling with Crook's troops.

The day before yesterday . . . the infantry picket saw about 50 Indians on the bluff opposite the camp, steeling two positions behind the rocks. The infantry fired upon them and the camp was alarmed. Though surprised they immediately returned the fire with yells. 100 flashes were instantly seen alone the crest of the ridge and several warriors road out in full view, circling rapidly; and there was instantly herd another sharp fusillade. . .

Half a mile up the river a band of Sioux tried to cross, but were driven back by the prompt attention of the pickets. Indians were seen at the same time at the south side of the camp but they remained distant.

A battalion, under the command of captain {Anson} mills, Third cavalry, advanced rapidly across the river, dismounted in a grove under the bluff and charged up the deep ravine. The first man to reach the top saw 200 Indians, moving incessantly on ponies, but slowly receding. The troops, stretching out in the skirmish line, drove them back in the face of a brisk fire. . .

It is supposed they had a large reserve massed in the ravines and expected to entice the small party into a pursuit, so as to surround and annihilate them. . . When they saw the full strength of the Cavalry they finally retreated.

VIEW OF BLUFF FROM CROOK'S CAMPSITE

WHAT'S THERE TODAY: The bluff where the Sioux and Cheyenne Indians made their show of force is clearly visible, as is the area where Crook made his campsite. Old cottonwood trees line the Tongue River, many of them probably old enough to have been there when the encounter took place.

ADDITIONAL INFORMATION: In January of 1877, Crazy Horse and Sitting Bull both camped with their followers in this vicinity. While camped here Crazy Horse would try to convince Sitting Bull to stay with him and continue their fight against the U.S. Army, but Sitting Bull had other plans. He was taking his people to Canada—the Grandmother's Land. This area is reportedly where Sitting Bull and Crazy horse would meet for the last time.

The bluffs are on private land; permission must be granted before accessing the area by the river and the bluffs.

There is no marker for this site, so be on the lookout for the bluffs northwest of where Prairie Dog Creek runs into the Tongue River.

Directions

Take Wyoming 336 (5th Street) east from Sheridan. At about 3 miles turn left onto Lower Prairie Dog Creek Road (County Road 1211). Follow the Creek on your right for 9 miles. The bluff is just west of where Prairie Dog Creek runs into the Tongue River.

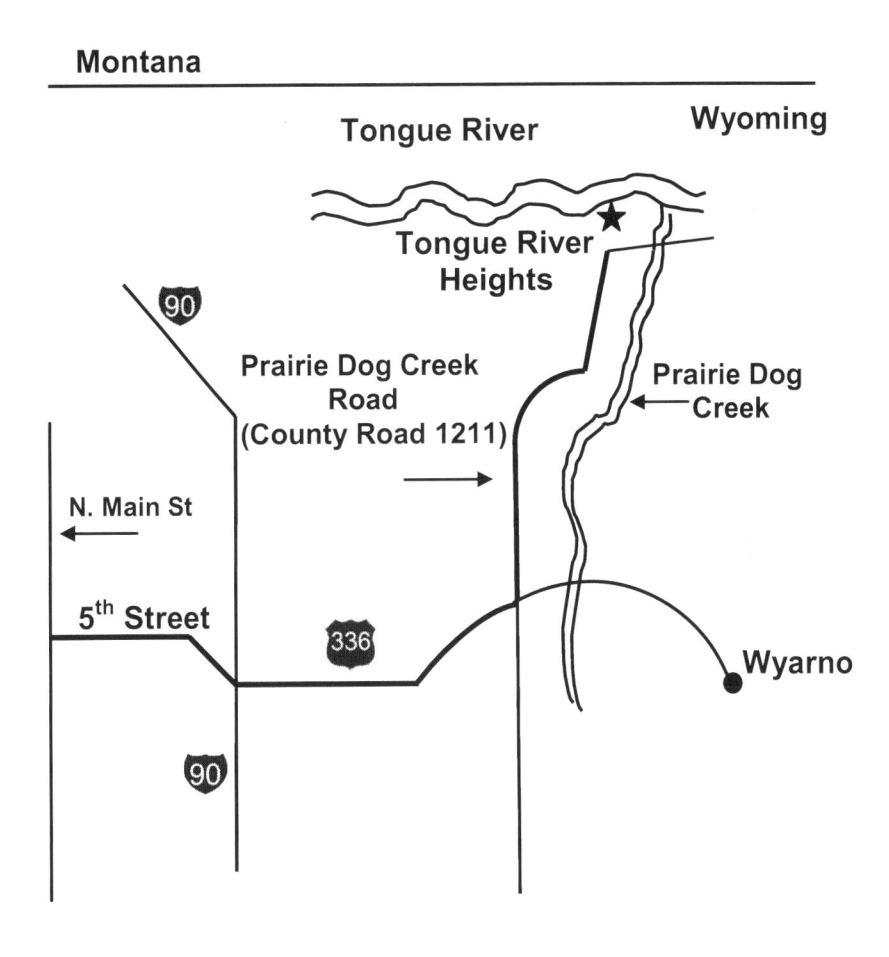

9

~Fort Phil Kearny~

History: Under the command of Colonel Henry B. Carrington, construction on Fort Phil Kearny (pronounced car-knee) began in July of 1866. It lay on a small plateau between the forks of Piney Creek, in the shadow of the Bighorn Mountains to the west.

Fort Phil Kearny, named after a famous Civil War General, was the largest of 3 forts (Reno and C.F. Smith were the others) established by the Army in the Powder River country to protect emigrant travelers along the Bozeman Trail.

The Sioux Indians, led by Red Cloud, viewed the building of the fort in the heart of their sacred hunting grounds as a threat to their very existence. The Indians were a constant menace in and around the fort, attacking wood trains headed for the pinery (5 miles west of the fort), and posing a danger to anyone leaving its protective walls.

During the fort's first six months, Indians killed over 150 persons, in addition to capturing 700 head of cattle, horses, and mules.

Despite the fact they were under constant siege from the Indians, those inside the fort (this included some women) tried to maintain as normal a life as possible. There was a sutler's store, laundress, hospital, even a 40 piece regimental band. It was home for some 400 soldiers and 150 civilians between 1866 and 1868.

The fort fueled Red Cloud's War which eventually led to Captain William J. Fetterman's entire command (80 men) being wiped out in December 1866 and the eventual closing of the fort.

> *I often wondered why a post so isolated was not swept away by a rush of mighty numbers of the surrounding savages, to avenge in one vast holocaust the invasion of their finest hunting grounds. Only our strong defenses prevented an assault, and the depletion of our numbers by attacks upon our exposed wood trains seemed to be their sole hope of finding some opportunity by which to find the way to final extermination of the garrison itself...*
>
> *Once indeed, Indians . . . crawled up close to the stockade, crawling under wolf-skins that covered their bodies, and a sentry was actually shot from the banquet that lay along the stockade, by an arrow, before any knowledge of the vicinity of the enemy came to the garrison.*
>
> Francis C. Carrington
Wife of Colonel Carrington
My Army Life and the Fort Phil Kearney Massacre

VIEW OF FORT AREA FROM PILOT HILL

WHAT'S THERE TODAY: Fort Phil Kearny was burned by the Indians when the Army abandoned it in 1868, however today's visitor is still able to walk the actual site. A map on the fort grounds gives a layout of where buildings once stood.

The old cemetery is just beyond the south boundary. While it's believed some civilian bodies are still buried there, the soldier's remains were disinterred in 1888 and reburied at the Little Bighorn Battlefield.

Looming behind the fort is Pilot Hill, where pickets were posted with big flags to warn of attacking Indians and signal the approach of wagon trains.

The ridgetop of the Sullivant Hills, directly in front of the fort, was used by wagons as the main road to the pinery, near present day Story, Wyoming. Just off to the northeast is Lodge Trail Ridge, which would play a major role in the Fetterman Fight (see next chapter) of Dec 21, 1866.

ADDITIONAL INFORMATION: The visitor's center has a small museum with artifacts from Fort Phil Kearny, as well as the Indian Wars. There is also an impressive model that shows what the fort looked like back in 1866.

Special programs are held at the fort during Bozeman Trail Days, usually the 2nd or 3rd weekend in June. There is also a special commemoration each December 21st on the anniversary of the Fetterman Fight. For more Fort info call **307.684.7629.**

WEBSITE: www.philkearny.vcn.com

CANNON AT FORT PHIL KEARNY

DIRECTIONS

I-90 east from Sheridan (about 20 miles), take exit 44 and follow the signs.

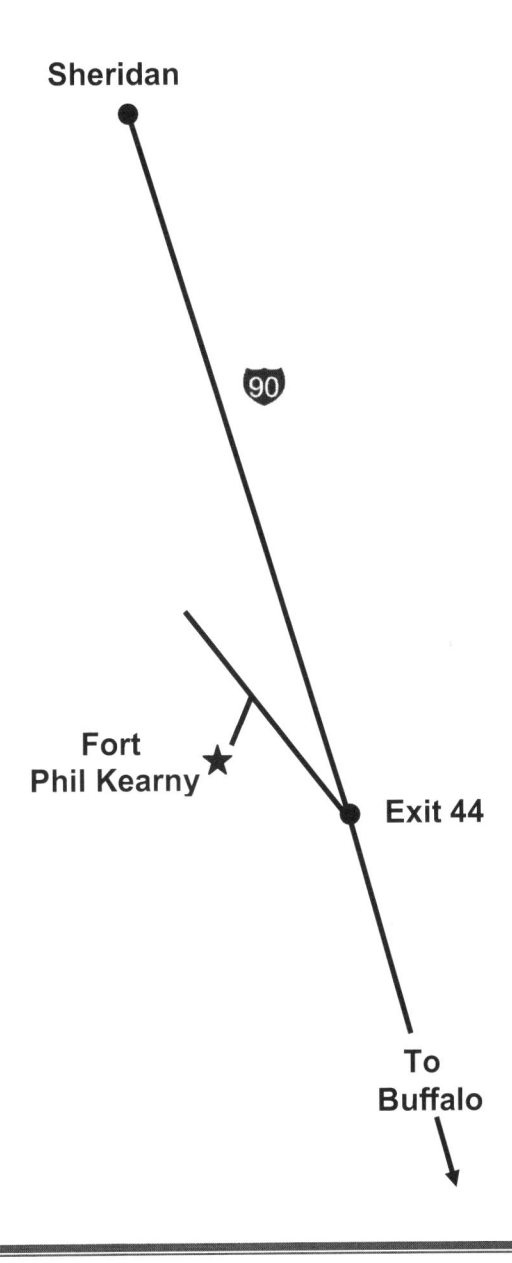

That's Here? Sheridan, WY

10

~Fetterman Battlefield~

History: Ten years before the Battle of the Little Bighorn and just 100 miles to the south, 80 men commanded by Captain William J. Fetterman were killed by Sioux, Cheyenne, and Arapaho warriors led by Red Cloud. For the U.S. Army there were no survivors. Fetterman met a horrible, prophetic death after once remarking, "with 80 men, I could ride through the whole Sioux nation."

On December 21, 1866, Fetterman's entire command was wiped out in less than an hour after it left the gates of nearby Fort Phil Kearny; all the soldier's bodies being mutilated with the exception of a young bugler. After the battle, Indian warriors praised the young soldier who used his bugle to fight for his life. The Sioux covered him in a buffalo hide to show their respect for his bravery.

The Indians lured the soldiers out of the fort that fateful day by attacking a wood train headed for the pinery. As Fetterman's command was about to leave the fort to give support, Colonel Henry Carrington ordered Fetterman not to pursue the Indians beyond Lodge Trail Ridge.

The Indians broke off their attack on the wood train as Fetterman's troops arrived and began a retreat towards Lodge Trail Ridge. Indian decoys led by Crazy Horse feigned Fetterman into pursuing them over the crest.

Now out of site from the fort, Crazy Horse and the other decoys continued to bait Fetterman and his men further away down a narrow ridge, where hidden in gullies and ravines on both sides were close to a thousand Sioux, Cheyenne, and Arapaho warriors. There were so many Indians that at one point they were actually killing each other with "friendly fire" from overshot arrows.

The Fetterman Battle was one of the worst defeats ever for the U.S. Army. If not for Custer's demise to some of these same Indians ten years later at the Battle of the Little Bighorn, many historians feel this would be the battle most people would be talking about and studying in great detail. As it is, most are not aware of it.

ROCKS WHERE FETTERMAN DIED

THIS TREE MAY HAVE WITNESSED THE BATTLE

WHAT'S THERE TODAY: With few exceptions, the battlefield remains almost as it did on December 21, 1866. A monument stands in the area where Fetterman retreated and eventually lost his life.

Along the ridgetop there is an old oak tree that some believe was alive to witness the fight. There is also an area known as the "Wheatley/Fisher Rocks" near the end of the ridge, where 2 civilians who were with the soldiers tried to fight off the Indians. There is a faded engraving on the rocks to mark their position.

A walking path winds through the battlefield posted with signs, pointing out areas of interest and giving details of the battle.

This is also one of the best areas to view ruts from the old Bozeman Trail.

ADDITIONAL INFORMATION: The battlefield is open every day, weather permitting. More information on the Fetterman Battle is available at the Fort Phil Kearny visitor's center nearby.

Guided tours are sometimes available, and each December 21, on the anniversary of the battle, a special commemoration is held at Fort Phil Kearny and on the Fetterman Battlefield.

For more info on the Fetterman Battlefield call **307.684.7629**.

WEBSITE: www.philkearny.vcn.com

Directions

I-90 east from Sheridan (about 20 miles), take exit 44 and follow the signs.

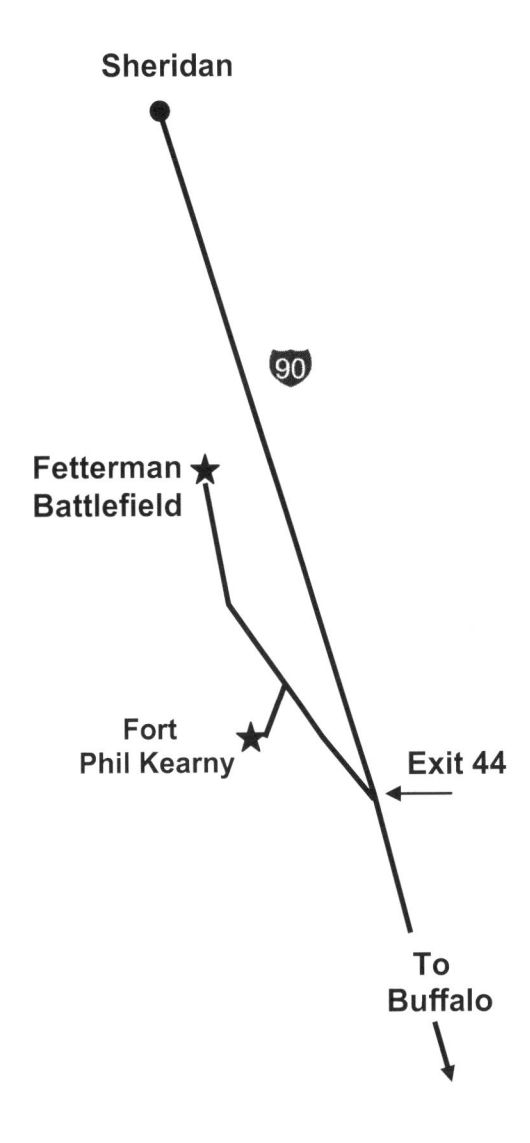

Sheridan

Fetterman Battlefield ★

Fort Phil Kearny ★

Exit 44

To Buffalo

11

~Wagon Box Fight~

History: On August 2, 1867, Company C of the 27th U.S. Infantry was attacked 6 miles west of Fort Phil Kearny (current day Story, Wyoming). Holed up inside a makeshift corral of wagon boxes, 26 soldiers and 6 civilians engaged nearly 800 Sioux and Cheyenne warriors. The battle is known as the Wagon Box Fight.

The soldiers were detailed to protect civilian woodcutters, who were securing wood for nearby Fort Phil Kearny. Upon arriving at the site just days before the battle, Captain James Powell ordered his men to take off the wooden boxes from their wagons and arrange them in an oval. Inside the enclosure they set up tents and stored up ammunition. This mini-fort saved their lives. Conditions inside the

REPLICA OF A WAGON BOX AT SITE

wagon box corral were dire during the battle. The hot August sun pounded the men from overhead, while Indian fire arrows ignited nearby grass and a manure pile. Soldiers and civilians at one point thought they might be overrun. Some removed their boots so they could pull the rifle trigger with their big toe, preparing to kill themselves rather than leaving it to the attacking Indians.

Led by Red Cloud, who oversaw the battle from the nearby hills, and Crazy Horse as a field leader on the ground, the Indian warriors were repelled by the soldiers who never seemed to stop firing. What the Indians didn't know was that Powell's men were equipped with new .50 caliber Springfield breech loading rifles. These had been ordered after the Fetterman Battle eight months before, where most of the soldiers had only single-shot muzzle loading rifles. These new rifles would prove to be the difference.

The Wagon Box Fight lasted almost 6 hours. The soldiers, despite being vastly outnumbered, lost only 3 men, with two wounded. Indian casualties that day were between 5 and 60 depending on the source. When reinforcements from Fort Phil Kearny arrived, the Indian warriors withdrew from the field.

This would be the last big engagement between troops at Fort Phil Kearny and the Indians led by Red Cloud. The Army would abandon Fort Phil Kearny the next summer and Red Cloud's War over forts along the Bozeman Trail came to an end.

WHAT'S THERE TODAY: It is a quiet, reflective area surrounded by the same hills where Red Cloud watched the battle and signaled directions to his warriors. Interpretive signs help describe the battle and show where events took place. There is a stone marker to dedicate the site, and a lone wagon box to show where the makeshift corral was setup.

> **ADDITIONAL INFORMATION:** The battlefield is open every day, weather permitting. More information on the Wagon Box Fight is available at the Fort Phil Kearny visitor's center nearby.
>
> Guided tours are sometimes given of the area. For more info call **307.684.7629**.

WEBSITE: www.philkearny.vcn.com

AREA OF THE WAGON BOX FIGHT

Directions

Take Interstate 90 east from Sheridan to Exit 44. Continue on the road past Fort Phil Kearny and follow the signs. **Note: The road is windy and narrow.** The Wagon Box Monument is roughly 5 miles from Fort Phil Kearny.

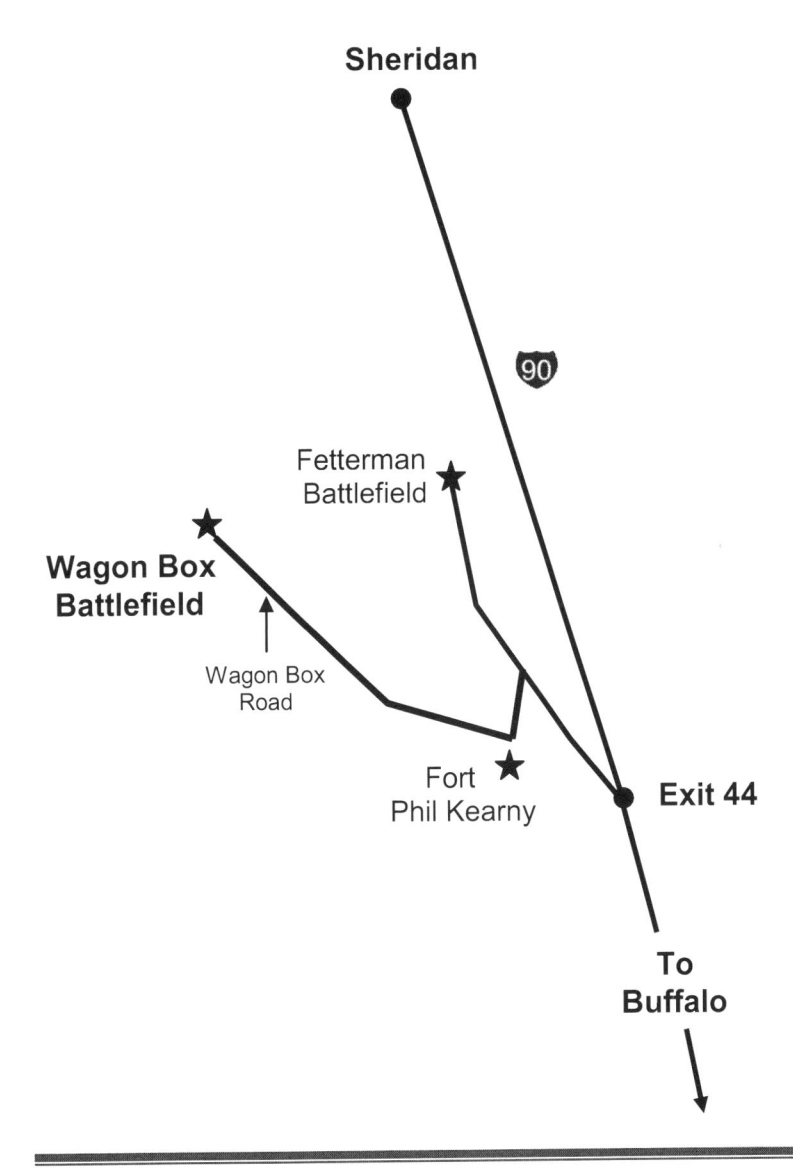

12

~Bozeman Trail~

HISTORY: The path was known and used by Indians for centuries, but it was John Bozeman who made it a common overland trail. Along with partner John Astor, they staked out The Bozeman Trail from the gold mines in Montana to Central, Wyoming. It was a shorter, more direct route, with better water than the alternate trails. It cut off from the Oregon Trail on the North Platte River (near present day Casper, Wyoming) and ran 500 miles to Virginia City, Montana.

On their first attempt to map out the route, Bozeman and Astor were attacked by Indians, but they were not dissuaded into giving up. Bozeman would lead the first civilian party up the trail in 1863, again being attacked by Indians who were not happy seeing wagon parties traipsing through their hunting grounds.

Traffic began to pick up on the trail following the Civil War, so in 1866 the U.S. Army built forts Reno, Phil Kearny, and C.F. Smith along the Bozeman Trail to protect civilian travelers from hostile Indians.

Sioux leader Red Cloud felt the Army had been dishonest in establishing the forts along the trail at the same time they were talking peace, so he recruited warriors and focused his wrath upon Fort Phil Kearny near present day Story, Wyoming. With the help of a young, upcoming warrior named Crazy Horse, Red Cloud harassed Fort Phil Kearny and the nearby Bozeman Trail using guerrilla war tactics, eventually wiping out the entire command (80 men) of Capt. William J. Fetterman.

The Army closed the fort soon after—the Indians then burned it to the ground—and the Bozeman Trail, for all practical purposes, was finished as a settler's route.

Only 3500 immigrants would travel the "Bloody" Bozeman Trail during its short and turbulent 5 years (1863-1868). It would later be opened again as a military road. General George Crook would use it in 1876 during the Great Sioux War to transport his men from Fort Fetterman (near Douglas, WY) up to the forks of Big and Little Goose Creek in present day Sheridan, Wyoming.

Today parts of Interstate 25 near Buffalo, Wyoming, and Interstate 90 from Buffalo to Sheridan are laid over the old ruts of the Bozeman Trail.

"In the middle of the afternoon the lead team . . . came rushing back with the alarm of Indians . . . They were armed with bows and arrows, and a few of them had guns, and some of them had long spears.

Ellen "Nellie" Gordon Fletcher
Diary entry on Bozeman Trail, 1866

THE BOZEMAN TRAIL RAN ALONG THIS RIDGE

WHAT'S THERE TODAY: There are places where the old trail ruts are still visible. One of the best places to view them is 20 miles south of Sheridan, on the site of the Fetterman Battlefield. Here you can actually stand in between them, while enjoying a view that is relatively unchanged from when they were being laid down over 145 years ago.

The Bozeman Trail can also be picked up between Ranchester and Dayton at the marker of the Sawyer Fight, although no ruts are visible at this location.

ADDITIONAL INFORMATION: You can learn more about the Bozeman Trail at Fort Phil Kearny near Story, Wyoming, as well as at the Bozeman Trail Museum in Big Horn, Wyoming.
For more info call **307.684.7629.**

WEBSITE: www.bozemantrail.org

Directions

About 20 miles south of Sheridan—take Exit 44 off of Interstate 90. The ruts can be seen on the Fetterman Battlefield, located about three miles from Fort Phil Kearny. Follow the signs.

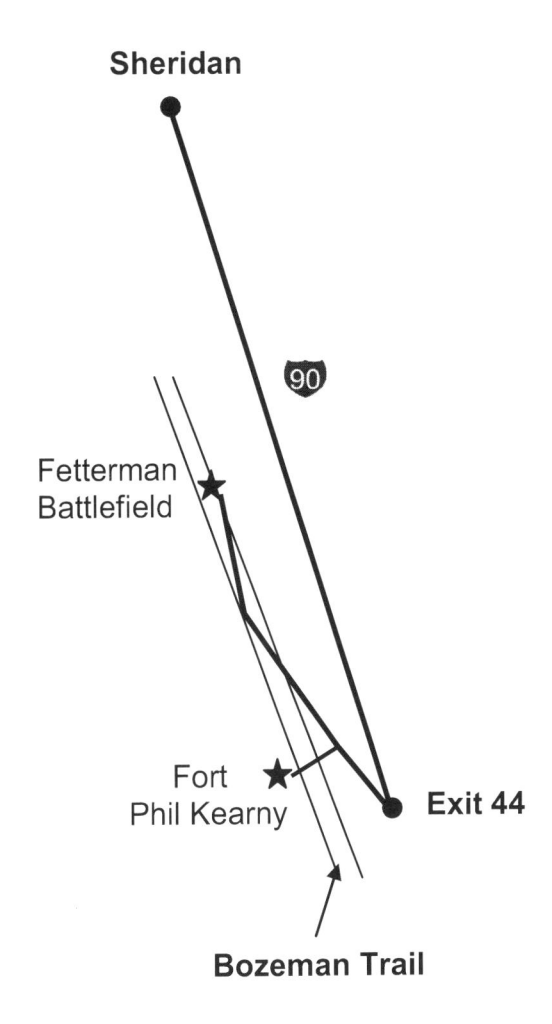

That's Here? Sheridan, WY

13

~Connor Battlefield~

History: The Battle of Tongue River began in the early morning hours of August 29, 1865. General Patrick Connor, leading the Army's Powder River Expedition, attacked the sleeping Arapaho Indian camp of Chief Black Bear along the Tongue River in present day Ranchester, Wyoming.

The warriors quickly sprang out of their buffalo hide beds and made a brief stand, allowing their women and children to flee upstream. Some of Connor's soldiers gave pursuit, while others stayed behind to ransack the village; burning up tipis and the Indian's food supplies they were storing up for the approaching winter. The Arapahos withdrew 10 miles up Wolf Creek before mounting a fierce counterattack. They drove the soldiers back to their campsite but were held at bay by two mounted howitzers.

Most reports put the Indian casualties at over 60, including Black Bear's son.

The Arapahos may have avoided Connor's soldiers altogether had they believed a Cheyenne warrior named Little Horse, who rode into their camp the day before with his young son and wife. They had seen Connor's troops on their journey and had rode fast to warn Black Bear's camp of the approaching soldiers. None of the Arapahos heeded Little Horse's warning, so he left, taking his son and wife a safe distance down the Tongue River.

Connor and his men were there that day to force the Indians into maintaining peace in the area. Following the Civil War, waves of white settlers were heading west. Most of these immigrants were using the Oregon and Bozeman Trails which cut right through the Indian's sacred hunting grounds. The Sioux and Cheyenne were upset by the intrusion, for the constant traffic of wagons and settlers were driving away the buffalo that they relied upon for food.

Many historians believe Connor's attack was instrumental in allying the non-hostile Arapaho with the Sioux and Cheyenne. The Arapaho attacked the Sawyer Expedition a few days later in the same area, and the following year they allied with the Sioux and Cheyenne at the Fetterman Fight, and again many years later at the Battle of the Little Bighorn.

TONGUE RIVER WHERE ARAPAHO WERE CAMPED

CONNOR BATTLEFIELD

WHAT'S THERE TODAY: Black Bear's encampment is now a quiet city park. Some of the old trees in the park were no doubt a part of the battle that took place next to the Tongue River, along where Black Bear's village was camped. There is a stone monument in the park dedicated to the battle and those that died there.

ADDITIONAL INFORMATION: The grounds are open year round, although vehicle access is prohibited from December thru April. There is a small daily use fee. Overnight camping is also available for a small fee.

For more info call **307-684-7629**.

WEBSITE: www.philkearny.vcn.com

DIRECTIONS

From Sheridan take I-90 west. Exit in Ranchester (Exit 9) and head west on Hwy 14 into Ranchester. Turn left on Gillette St. Follow the signs.

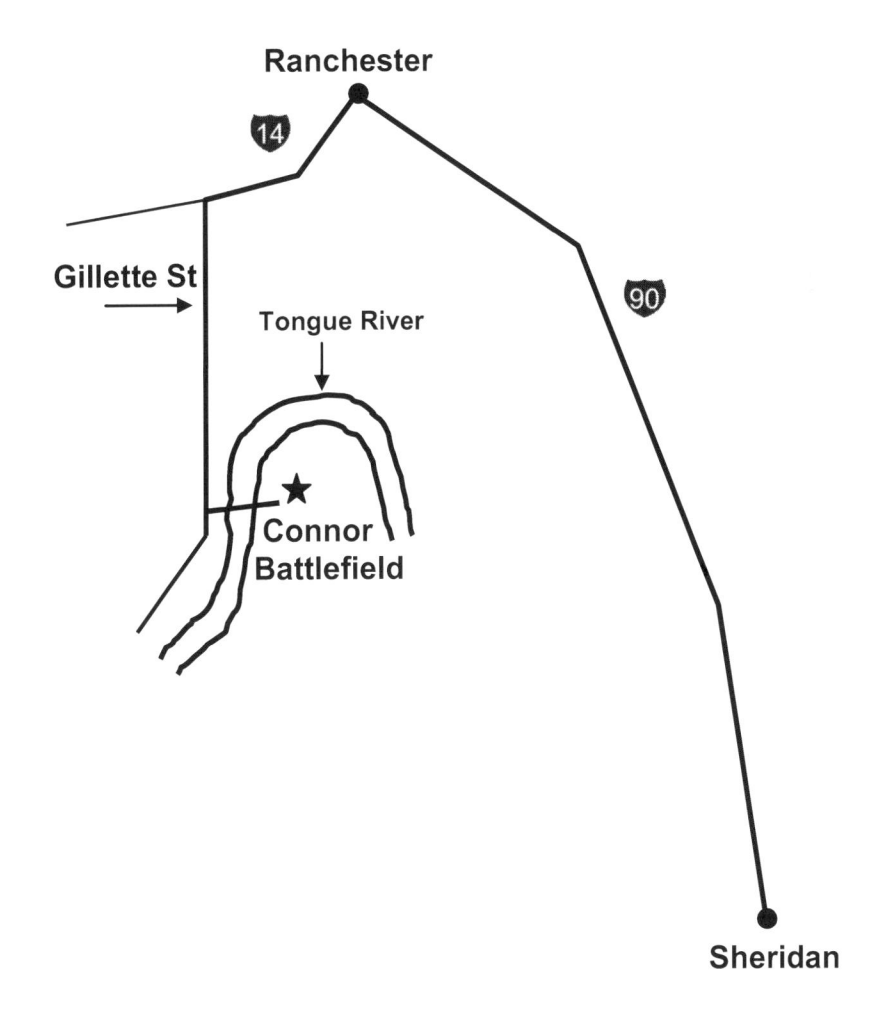

14

~Sawyer Fight~

HISTORY: On August 31, 1865, 2 days after General Patrick Connor and his Powder River Expedition wiped out Black Bear's small Arapaho village along the Tongue River, a surveying party led by Colonel James Sawyer came moving thru the area. The 82 wagon party was engineering a route from Sioux City, Iowa, to the gold fields of Montana using the Bozeman Trail.

The Arapaho, still smarting over the Connor assault, were looking for revenge. Warriors ambushed the train where the Bozeman Trail cut across the Tongue River between present day Ranchester and Dayton, Wyoming. Arapaho warriors attacked scouts out ahead of the party first, while others stampeded the train's cattle in the rear.

Two weeks earlier the same train had been harassed by the Sioux and the Cheyenne back near the Powder River.

Despite the fact that they were low on ammunition after the fight with Connor, the Arapaho were able to hold the surveying train down for thirteen days. Three in the Sawyer party were killed. The party finally retreated back towards Fort Reno, and was eventually met by Connor's troops who escorted them back through the area.

> *The Indians devined our motive and attempted to cut off our retreat. . . . Twenty five Indians circumvented the train and rode ahead to a vantage point along a high bank. . . James Dilliner, driving an oxen team in the lead, was killed by a bullet which struck him in the back, and in a few minutes, E.G. Merrill, an emigrant of Sioux Falls, was also killed by a bullet while standing near the wheels of his wagon.*
>
> Albert M Holman
> *Eyewitness to the Indian Wars, 1865-1890*

AREA OF SAWYER FIGHT

BOZEMAN TRAIL MARKER NEAR THE SAWYER FIGHT

WHAT'S THERE TODAY: The site is marked by a sign giving information and pointing out areas of the fight. In the 1860s, the Bozeman Trail crossed the highway about where the sign is today.

At one point in the late 1800's there was a stage station and small post office near the area, but they, along with the Bozeman Trail, have since given way to alfalfa fields and prairie.

ADDITIONAL INFORMATION: The Sawyer Fight and The Connor Battlefield are only minutes apart. Also nearby is the Tongue River. It was near this area next to the Tongue River that Crazy Horse and Sitting Bull reportedly camped for a time during the fall of 1875.

WEBSITE: www.wyomingtalesandtrails.com/ftkearney.html

DIRECTIONS

From Sheridan take I-90 west to Ranchester. Exit US Hwy 14W. The road sign pointing out the Sawyer Fight is on Hwy 14W between the towns of Ranchester and Dayton (about 3 miles east of Dayton).

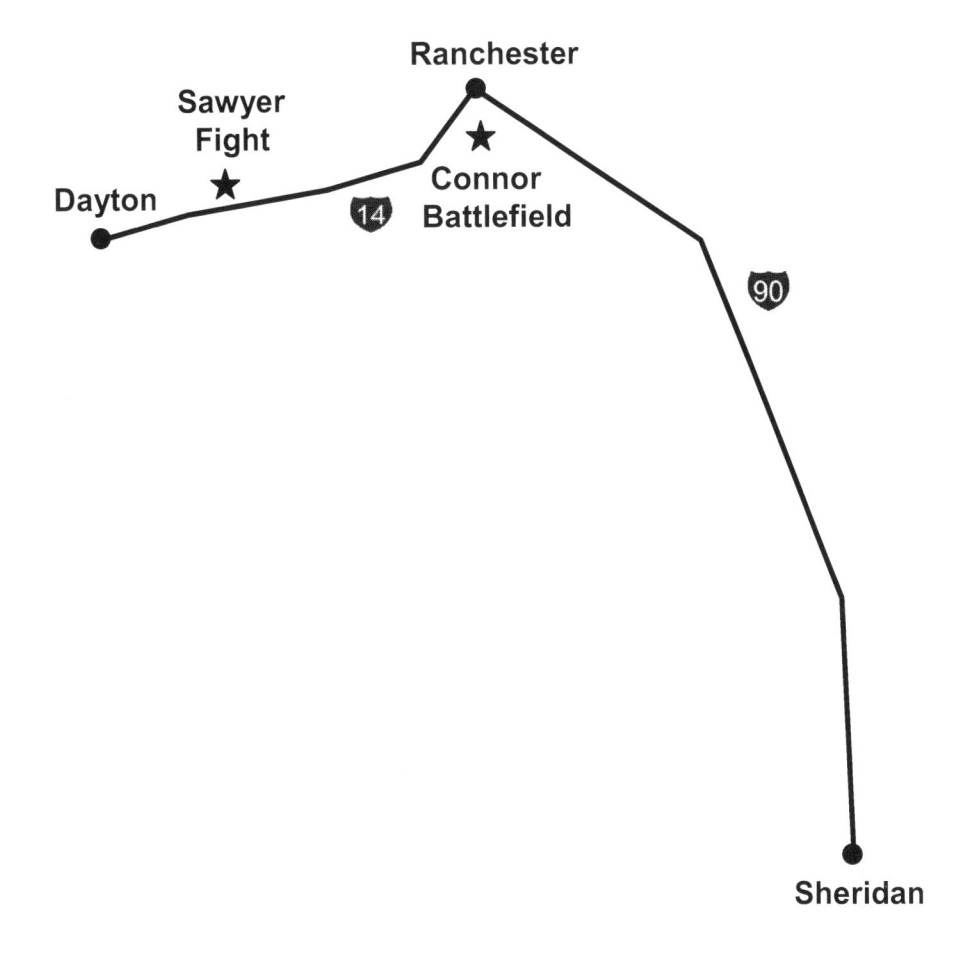

15

~Tongue River~

History: The Tongue River is a tributary of the Yellowstone River that flows in southern Montana. It makes its way out of the Bighorn Mountains near Dayton, Wyoming (23 miles from Sheridan), and meanders across ranchland and prairie until it finally reaches the Yellowstone near Miles City, Montana. Scholars disagree as to how the Tongue got its name. Some believe it derives its name from the many tongue-like buttes that line the river; others believe it came from a rock formation resembling a tongue that overlooks the river near where it flows out of the Bighorn Mountains.

During the 1800's the Tongue was an important river for the area's Plains Indians, providing a source of food and water. It was along the Tongue in northern Wyoming and southern Montana where the Sioux and Cheyenne Indians often made their winter camps. Along the Tongue just north of present day Sheridan, Wyoming, is where Red Cloud established villages during Red Cloud's War. This is where they headquartered their main camps, while warriors traveled some 30 miles south to harass soldiers at Fort Phil Kearny.

It is said that some Indian camps along the Tongue were at times so big that it took a rider a full day on horseback to ride from one side of the encampment to the other.

In October of 1875, Crazy Horse and Sitting Bull are reported to have camped along the Tongue River near present day Dayton, Wyoming. Crazy Horse and Sitting Bull would also meet for the very last time along the Tongue River near the Montana/Wyoming border in early 1877.

Many battles during the Indian Wars were fought along the Tongue. General Patrick Connor ransacked the Arapaho village of Black Bear in 1865 along the Tongue in present day Ranchester, Wyoming. Two days after the Connor battle, a party of surveyors was attacked (Sawyer Fight) just after it had forded the Tongue between present day Ranchester and Dayton, Wyoming. And The Skirmish at Tongue River Heights took place 3 weeks before the Battle of the Little Bighorn, where the Tongue meets up with Prairie Dog Creek near the Wyoming/Montana border.

A couple of weeks after the Battle of the Little Bighorn, General George Crook sent Lt. Frederick W. Sibley out on a scout to see if they could locate hostile Indians. While moving along the Tongue River near present day Dayton, Wyoming, the patrol was discovered by a party of Sioux and Cheyenne warriors. They were chased into the Bighorn Mountains, where they were forced to abandon their horses and hike some 30 miles back to their base camp along Big Goose Creek.

Today the Tongue River is a spot for fishing enthusiasts and kids floating on inner tubes on hot summer days. If the old trees could talk imagine the stories they would have to tell of the great Indian encampments that used to spread out under their shady branches.

WHAT'S THERE TODAY: The Tongue River is accessible in many spots around Sheridan, Wyoming. The area where Crook's troops encountered Sioux and Cheyenne warriors near the Montana/Wyoming border (The Skirmish at Tongue River Heights) is about 5 miles east of Sheridan. This is the approximate area where Crazy Horse and Sitting Bull had their final meeting before Sitting Bull led his followers to Canada.

In Ranchester, Wyoming, you can walk along the Tongue River where General Patrick Connor's troops attacked the village of Black Bear. And just north of Sheridan you can fish along the Tongue where the Plains Indians often made their camps.

ADDITIONAL INFORMATION: Tongue River Canyon near Dayton, Wyoming, (23 miles northwest of Sheridan) is a popular hiking trail. There is also a cave that can be explored near the beginning of the trailhead. Tongue River Reservoir in southern Montana (just across the Wyoming/Montana border) is a popular boating and camping area.

TREES LINE THE TONGUE RIVER NEAR WYOMING/MONTANA BORDER

DIRECTIONS

I-90 crosses the Tongue River just north of Sheridan (Exit 14, Acme). Montana Hwy 314 accesses Tongue River near Decker, Montana. Also take I-90 west to WY-339 (Exit 16 at Port of Entry) and go east. Turn left onto Decker Hwy 338 which becomes MT-314 and you can access the Tongue near Tongue River Reservoir.

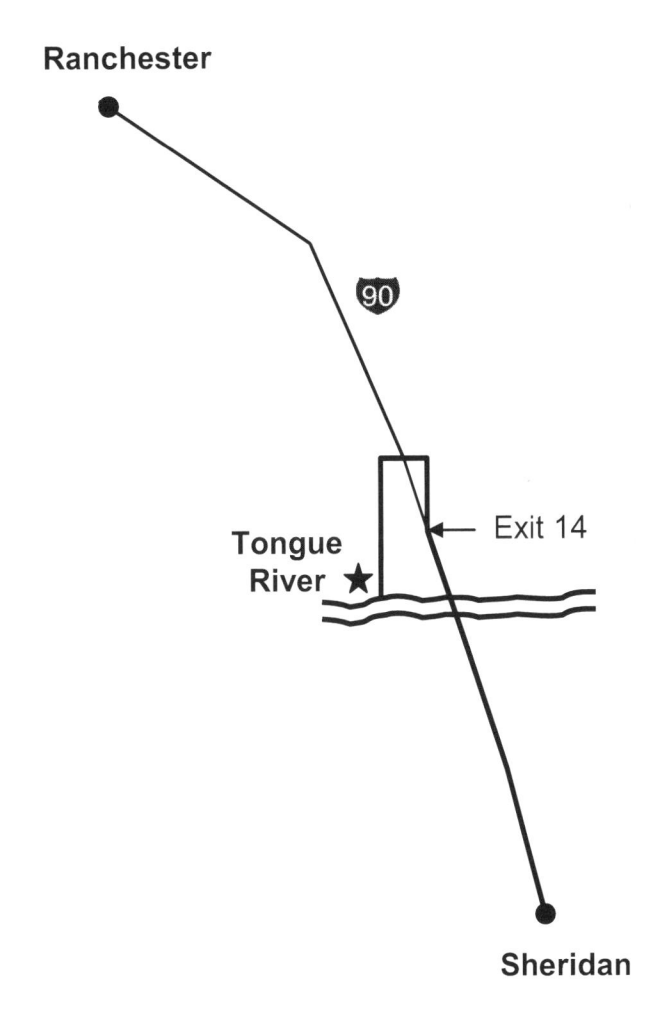

Bonus Site

Lake DeSmet

Between Buffalo and Sheridan on the east side of Interstate 90 is Lake DeSmet. It is named for Jesuit priest Pierre-Jean De Smet, who was active in missionary work with various Indian tribes in the 1800's.

For immigrants and the military, Lake DeSmet signaled the approach of Fort Phil Kearny for wagon trains along the Bozeman Trail; while for the Plains Indians, who called it "Medicine Lake", it held special spiritual significance. Many Indians sought the lake for vision quests and other religious ceremonies. Crazy Horse reportedly had a life-changing vision at Lake DeSmet.

The lake was much smaller in those days. It has since been enlarged and today is a reservoir serving the area's water needs, along with being a boating and recreation haven in the summer and an ice fisherman's paradise in the winter.

Buffalo, Wyoming

16

~Buffalo, Wyoming~

History: Buffalo, Wyoming, owes its beginnings to Fort McKinney which the Army established next to the Bighorn Mountains in 1878. Soon after the construction of Fort McKinney, civilian contractors and businessman began to move in to make money from the soldiers stationed there. Later, when a nearby trading post relocated next to Clear Creek just down from the fort, a little establishment began to quickly spring up.

As the small settlement continued to grow, they decided it needed a name. Nominations were written on slips of paper and placed into a hat. Buffalo was the name drawn out, suggested by a man who had come west from Buffalo, New York.

Soon, the new town of Buffalo became a mix of cattlemen, miners, and sheepherders. Cattle barons moved in large herds during

FORT MCKINNEY GROUNDS

the 1800s, but over time they found themselves becoming crowded out by settlers from the east, looking to claim land under the Homestead Act.

By 1892, these wealthy cattle barons, under the name of the Wyoming Stock Growers Association, sought to exterminate the homesteaders, and Buffalo found itself in the middle of a range war that would become known as the Johnson County War.

The Wyoming Stock Growers Association hired a group of Texas gunman—who called themselves the Regulators—and came up with a list of 70 ranchers they planned to eliminate.

After debarking from a special train in Casper, Wyoming, the Regulators made their way towards Buffalo, cutting telegraph wires along the way. Their first target was Nate Champion, a small rancher near present day Kaycee, Wyoming. They shot Champion after forcing him out of his cabin when they set fire to it.

The Regulators moved on towards Buffalo, where they were met at the T.A. Ranch just south of town by an outraged posse of Buffalo citizens. The Regulators were pinned down inside a barn, and had to be rescued by the military from nearby Fort McKinney.

Today Buffalo is a quiet community; a gateway for travelers between Mount Rushmore and Yellowstone National Park.

WHAT'S THERE TODAY: Many of the historic buildings in downtown Buffalo still remain. The Occidental Hotel provides a look at the past, where you can visit a real Old West saloon and walk through rooms where famous names like Butch Cassidy and the Sundance Kid, author Owen Wister, Calamity Jane and President Roosevelt all stayed.

The Johnson County Courthouse in the center of town is one of the oldest structures still standing in Wyoming.

On Main Street you'll find a small curve in the road just down from the Occidental Hotel. It is said that back in the late 1870s, one of the local merchants felt he was getting short changed on the number on customers coming into the fast growing settlement. So, the merchant decided to take matters into his own hands. He found a friend with a bull team and they changed the dirt path to go by his store. The curve in the road remains there today.

Clear Creek still runs through the middle of town, right next to the Occidental Hotel where the town of Buffalo began.

Fort McKinney (2 miles west of Buffalo on Hwy 16) is now the Veteran's Home of Wyoming. Two buildings remain from the original fort: the hospital and dairy.

> **ADDITIONAL INFORMATION:** The Jim Gatchell Museum is a must see if you're in town between May and mid-October. The museum displays a number of artifacts from the Indian Wars, pieces from Johnson County history and the Johnson County War, as well as artifacts from the Battle of the Little Bighorn.
>
> The Occidental Hotel also houses a museum with artifacts and pictures from Buffalo's past.
>
> There are a number of historic buildings throughout downtown Buffalo, many of them dating back to the late 1800s.
>
> For more info call **307.684.5544.**

WEBSITE: www.buffalowyo.org

DIRECTIONS

I-90 East from Sheridan for about 31 miles. Merge onto I-25 South. Take exit 299 (US Hwy 16) and go right. Turn left onto Main Street.

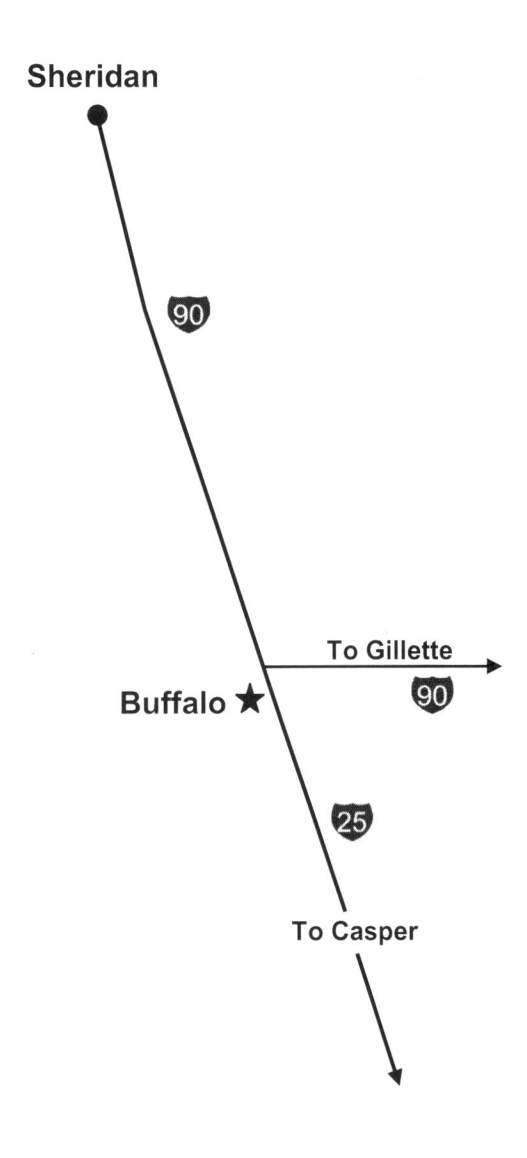

17

~Occidental Hotel~

History: What started out in a tent 130 years ago is still alive and well in downtown Buffalo, Wyoming. The Occidental Hotel is a piece of living history next to Clear Creek where it began in 1879. Butch Cassidy and the Sundance Kid, Owen Wister (author of *The Virginian*), Ernest Hemingway, and Presidents Herbert Hoover and Teddy Roosevelt all stayed there. And legendary Old West character Tom Horn spent many an hour in the Occidental's saloon.

In 1880, the hotel became a permanent structure as a log cabin, with six rooms, a lobby, and a saloon. Around the turn of the century, it was remodeled when Clear Creek twice flooded its bank, becoming the block long brick hotel that it is today.

During its heyday in the late 1800's and early 1900's, the Occidental Hotel was the social and political center of Johnson County. There was a saloon, card and billiard rooms, a barbershop, and restaurant. Rooms went for $2.50. There was many a meeting in the saloon and the upstairs rooms to discuss the Johnson County War and local politics.

As with a lot of businesses during the Great Depression in the 1930's, the Occidental began to decline. Money was in short supply and guests became scarce.

Business would pick up again during World War II, but after the war a new kind of roadside industry would begin to take customers away from the Occidental—motels. By the 1970's and 1980's, the Occidental had resorted to renting out its rooms as apartments.

The hotel would close its doors in 1986. By the late 90's there was talk of tearing down the historic building. New owners came in 1997 and rescued the aging hotel. They began a ten year restoration of the old hotel, returning it to its original splendor.

Today the Occidental is a thriving hotel where guests are able to come and stay, and still taste a little of the Old West.

OCCIDENTAL HOTEL LOBBY

WHAT'S THERE TODAY: The Occidental Hotel has been restored to its grandeur of the early 1900's. Look close and you might even find some original bullet holes in the ceiling. There is a hotel museum with pictures and artifacts from Buffalo's past, and you can walk through rooms where famous names from American history have stayed.

The lobby is adorned with period furniture from the hotel's heyday and the embossed ceilings are original, as is the bar in the hotel's saloon.

ADDITIONAL INFORMATION: The Occidental Hotel is a working hotel with rooms available year round. The hotel restaurant is named after Owen Wister's novel *The Virginian*. Some believe the climatic gunfight at the end of the novel takes place just outside the Occidental on Main Street. It is believed that Wister came across some ideas for his book while spending time at the Occidental in 1885.

The Occidental was named *Best Hotel in the West* by True West magazine in 2007 and 2008.

For more info call **307.684.0451**.

WEBSITE: www.occidentalwyoming.com

OCCIDENTAL SALOON

Directions

I-90 East from Sheridan for about 31 miles. Merge onto I-25 South. Take exit 299 (Hwy 16) and go right. Turn left onto Main Street.

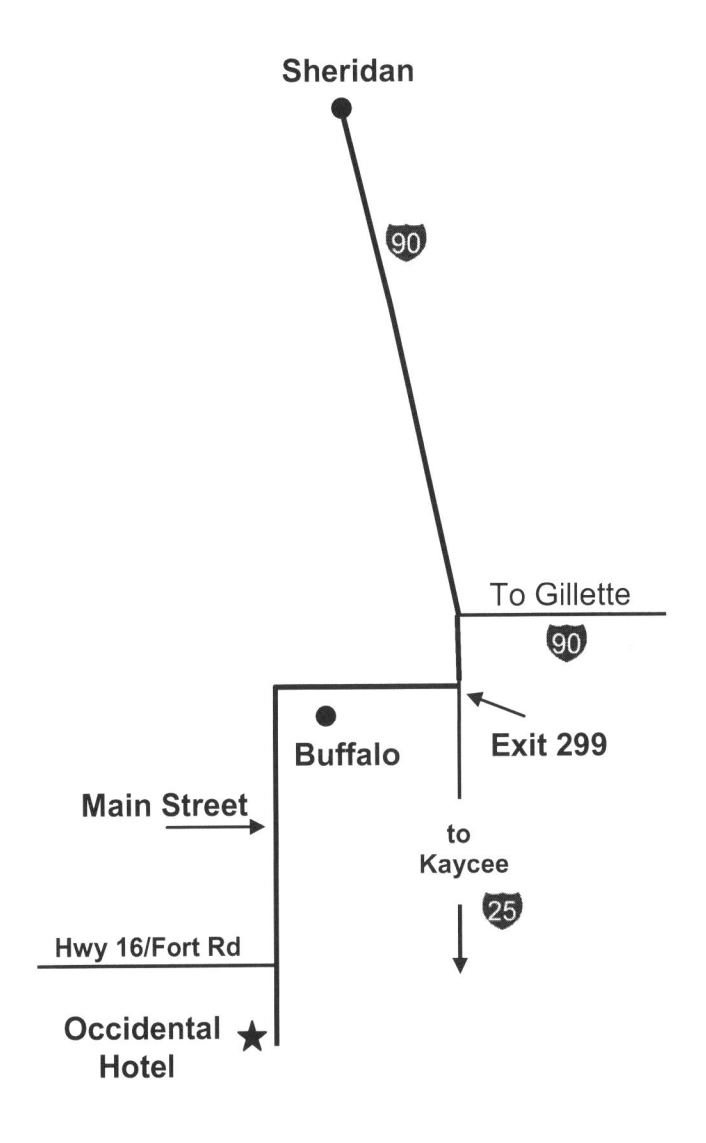

Up the Road

Bonus Site

The Mill Inn

Today it's a hotel with business offices, but when it was built in 1920, it was Wyoming's largest and most modern flour mill, turning out 1,000 barrels of flour a day.

Bakers from all over the country used flour made in Sheridan, Wyoming, at the Sheridan Flour Mills, Inc, as it was called then.

In 1927, the mill was upgraded with an additional 10 concrete grain feed storage tanks that are still standing on the site today. At its peak the mill employed 75 people with an annual payroll of $350,000.

Sheridan Flour Mills, Inc. sold the mill in 1963 to the Nebraska Consolidated Mill Company who closed it in 1974 due to climbing freight rates for grain and flour. The buildings and land were sold off and remolded into the 44-room hotel and office spaces you see today.

2161 Coffeen Ave. 307.672.6401

18

~Big Horn, Wyoming~

History: It is said that Frank James once used the area as a hideout, and for years the Crow and Sioux Indians called the area home, until the Bozeman Trail brought the white man in the 1860's. Oliver Hanna became its first settler in 1878, and would operate Big Horn's first hotel—The Oriental—across from where the Big Horn Mercantile is today.

At one time Big Horn was the hub of the region, with a population larger than Sheridan. It had a small college, brick factory, and newspaper. It made a bid to be the seat of Sheridan County in 1888, but lost in a run-off election. When the railroad came to Sheridan in 1892, Big Horn began to lose many of its residents to the burgeoning town.

In the early 1890's, Scottish brothers Malcolm and William Moncrieffe moved to the area and began buying up horses for the

British army. They shipped nearly 20,000 horses from Big Horn to Africa for the British to use in the Boer Wars.

The Moncrieffe brothers also established a sheep operation raising Rambouillet and Corriedale breeding sheep.

In 1898, Malcolm Moncrieffe brought the sport of polo to Big Horn when he built one of the first Polo fields west of the Mississippi. World class polo players from all over the globe now come to Big Horn, Wyoming, to enjoy polo with the Bighorn Mountains as a backdrop.

Englishman Oliver Henry Wallop, the second son of the 5th Earl of Portsmouth, found his way to Big Horn about the same time as the Moncrieffes. Wallop also ran horses and bought the Canyon Ranch near Little Goose Canyon where Buffalo Bill Cody and President Teddy Roosevelt came to stay as guests. Wallop's grandson, Malcolm, would eventually become a U.S. Senator.

At one time 1000 residents resided in Big Horn. Today there are just over 200.

BIGHORN MOUNTAINS OUTSIDE BIG HORN, WY

BOZEMAN TRAIL MUSEUM

WHAT'S THERE TODAY: Some of the buildings still in use today in Big Horn date back to the 1800's. The Bozeman Trail Museum is located in a restored blacksmith's shop built around 1880. Just down the street from the museum are the Bozeman Trail Inn and the Mercantile, both of which were in use back in the town's early days.

ADDITIONAL INFORMATION: The Bozeman Trail ran through the area where Big Horn is today.

The Bradford Brinton Museum, Big Horn Equestrian Center, and Flying H Polo Ranch are all located in the vicinity.

Queen Elizabeth II of England stayed with relatives at the Wallop Ranch in Big Horn on her visit to America in 1984.

The Bozeman Trail Museum is typically open weekends, Memorial Day thru Labor Day. For more info call **307.674.6363**.

WEBSITE: www.visitsheridanwyoming.com
www.sheridanwyoming.org

Directions

From downtown Sheridan take Coffeen Ave south. Coffeen turns into US Hwy 335. Go 7 miles. From I-90 take Exit 25 in Sheridan. Go West to Coffeen/US 335. Turn left and go 7 miles.

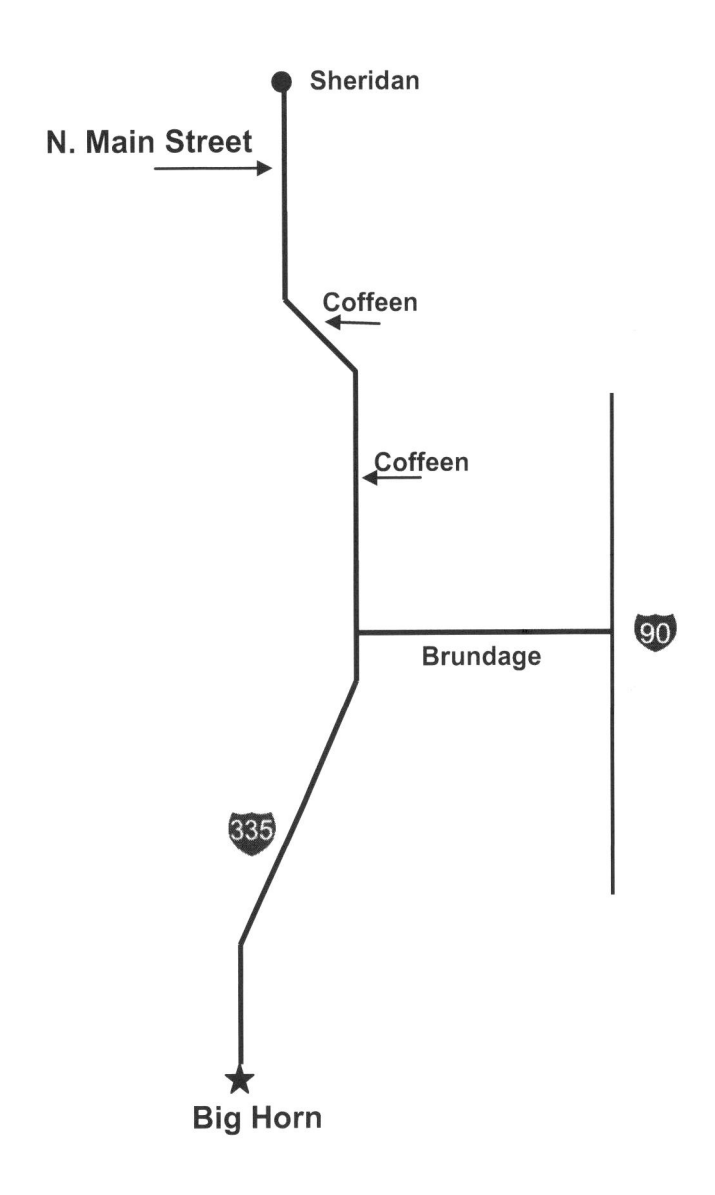

19

~BRADFORD BRINTON MEMORIAL~

HISTORY: The Bradford Brinton Memorial began as a working cattle ranch back in 1892. It was called the Quarter Circle A Ranch then, started by Scotsman William Moncrieffe, who along with his brother, Malcolm, was responsible for establishing the sport of polo in the Sheridan area.

In 1923, Moncrieffe sold the main house along with some land to Bradford Brinton, a Yale educated engineer who served under General Pershing in Mexico and World War I.

Brinton remodeled the main house, using it primarily as a vacation home with his wife, Catherine, and twin daughters, Pat and Barbara. Inside he deposited his collection of western art featuring originals from Frederick Remington and Charles M. Russell. He also had an extensive collection of rare books, along with an original letter from Abraham Lincoln and a George Washington document.

When Brinton died in 1936, he left the property to his sister, Helen, who kept the home and her brother's collection, even having some of his art and objects shipped out from his New York City Park Avenue apartment.

Helen Brinton would use the house mainly as a summer home until her death in 1960. She left the house and land in care of the Northern Trust Company of Chicago, who still runs it today.

WHAT'S THERE TODAY: The Ranch Foreman's house—the original structure on the land—still survives just north of the main house. The main house that you see today is the remodeled version from 1927-28. It features period furniture from the time and original paintings from Remington, Russell, and Hans Kleiber.

Lining the road outside the house are several rock walls that Helen had built to keep the ranch employees working after the livestock were sold off, following her brother's (Bradford) death.

Next to the house is a museum, featuring paintings from Charles Russell and Frederic Remington. There are also a number of Indian artifacts on display, as is the original letter written by Abraham Lincoln and the George Washington document mentioned above.

ADDITIONAL INFORMATION: In the movie Broken Trail, this is the ranch Robert Duvall drives his horse herd to from Oregon. The grounds are open Memorial Day through Labor Day. Visitors can tour the main house and stroll the existing grounds.

For more info call **307.672.3173**.

WEBSITE: www.bbmandm.org

TIPI AT BRADFORD BRINTON

Directions

From downtown Sheridan take Coffeen Ave south. Coffeen turns into US Hwy 335. Go about 10 miles (3 miles past Big Horn) and follow signs.

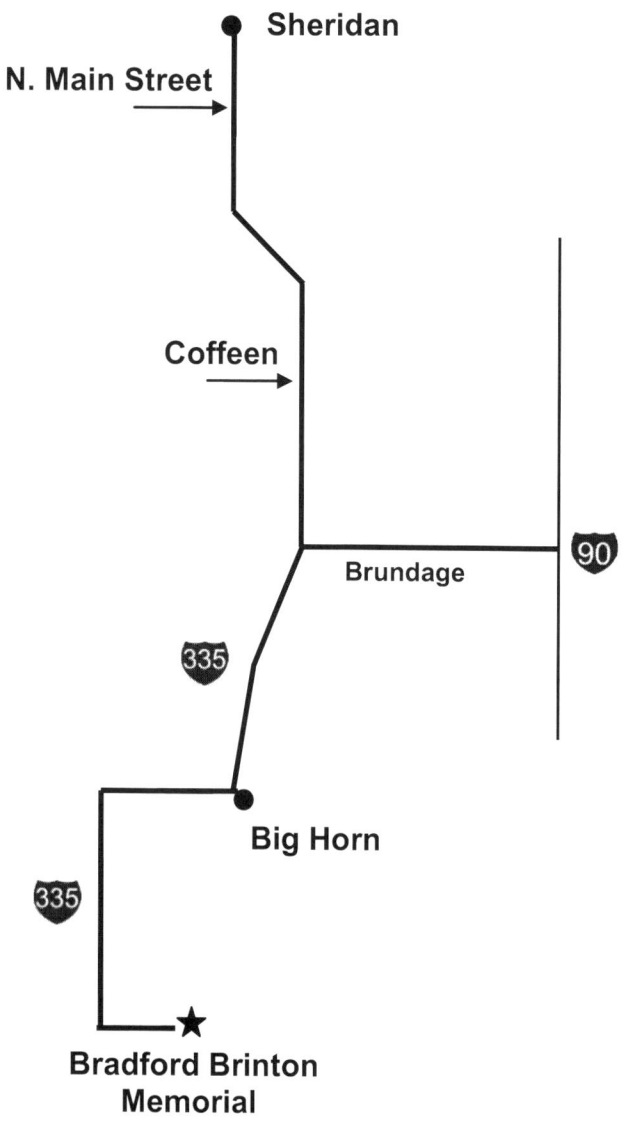

Bonus Site

Don King Museum

If you are an Old West history buff, one of Sheridan's hidden gems is the Don King Museum behind King's Saddlery.

Established in 1989, the unassuming warehouse is home to an extensive collection of cowboy memorabilia, as well as some 500 saddles, many crafted by Don King himself (King was a world renowned saddlemaker. He has other saddles on display at the National Cowboy Hall of Fame and the PRCA Rodeo Hall of Fame).

The museum also displays a wide array of western guns, Native American artifacts, a saddle belonging to Gene Autry, and be on the lookout for the buckskin pants worn by John Wayne in the movie *Red River*.

If there is only place you can visit while in Sheridan, make sure it is the Don King Museum!

184 N. Main Street. 307.672.2702

20

~Dayton, Wyoming~

History: Once the Indian Wars ended in 1877, homesteaders slowly began to settle the area around the Tongue River in Northeastern, Wyoming. The town of Dayton sprang up soon after, named in 1882 for 21 year-old Joseph Dayton Thorn, who had moved to the area with his mother from Colorado. The town boasted 16 people at that time and Thorn would eventually become a prominent banker in the town.

The arrival of the railroad in 1896 brought more settlers to the area, along with a lucrative industry: railroad ties and timber.

Elaborate flumes were built up in the Bighorn Mountains to carry the freshly cut trees 26 miles down to the Tongue River in Dayton.

They were then floated down the Tongue to the Big Horn Timber Co mill in Ranchester, Wyoming.

While Dayton is a rather isolated community, it has managed to lead the state in some important areas. Wyoming's first female mayor (she was arguably the first female mayor in the U.S.), Susan Wissler, would serve Dayton from 1911-1915. And just outside of Dayton, Howard Eaton established the first dude ranch in Wyoming (and possibly the first in the country) in 1904 on Wolf Creek. Dayton is also credited with holding one of the first formal rodeos in the state of Wyoming in the early 1890's.

Painter Hans Kleiber made his home in Dayton from 1923 until his death in 1967. Kleiber's prints are known around the world, especially among collectors of sporting and nature prints.

The Dayton area is also a favorite for hang glider enthusiasts who converge on Sand Turn just above the town every Memorial Day and Labor Day weekend.

Today the town of Dayton remains a small community, sitting quietly at the base of the Bighorn Mountains. Its population at this printing is around 700 people.

BIGHORN MOUNTAINS NEAR DAYTON, WY

WHAT'S THERE TODAY: The Dayton Mercantile building still resides on Main Street, a leftover from the town's earlier days. Next door to the Mercantile is Susan Wissler's house, constructed in 1885.

The Hans Kleiber Studio Museum is also on Main Street. The studio looks very much like it did in Kleiber's time, with his furniture, books, and art supplies all on display. The museum is open during the summer months.

The Tongue River flows nearby on the edge of town through Dayton City Park. The park is home to the Dayton Bell Tower, which was used at one time by firefighters as a watchtower and a place to hang their hoses to dry. It was also used as a plane lookout after the bombing of Pearl Harbor.

ADDITIONAL INFORMATION: Eaton's Ranch is still along Wolf Creek about ten miles outside of Dayton. It was used in the filming of the movie *Flicka* in 2006 starring Tim McGraw, and *Wild Horses* with Kenny Rogers in 1985.

For more info on Dayton, WY, call **307.655.2217**.

WEBSITE: www.daytonwyoming.org

DAYTON MERCANTILE

DIRECTIONS

Take I-90 west to Ranchester, WY (Exit 9, US Hwy 14W). Go about 6 miles west on US Hwy 14W to Dayton.

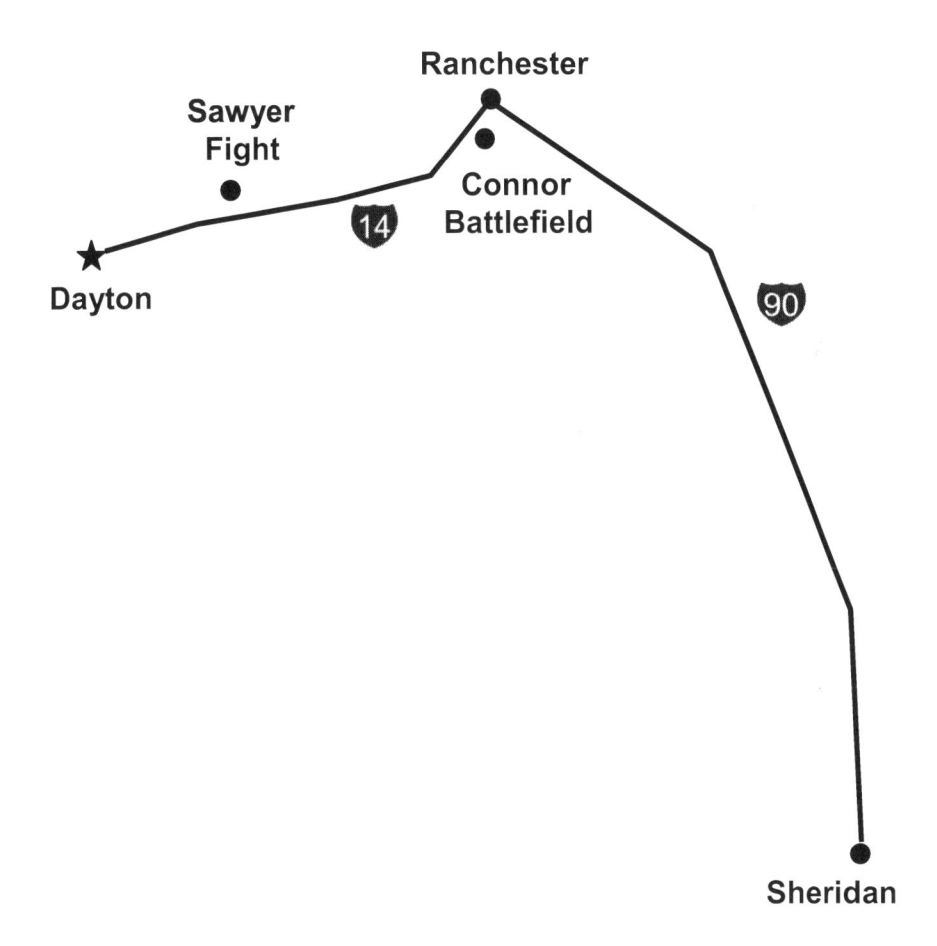

WITHIN A

3 HOUR DRIVE

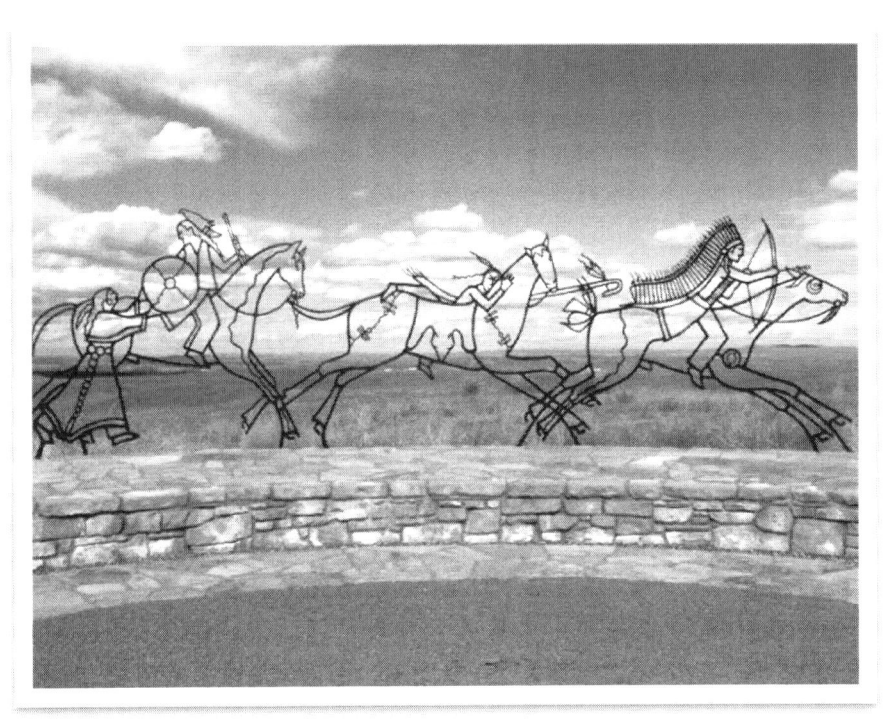

INDIAN MEMORIAL AT LITTLE BIGHORN BATTLEFIELD

21

~Battle of the Little Bighorn~

History: It may be American history's most famous battle. Countless movies have been made about it, and even today new books debate what transpired there. Known to many as Custer's Last Stand, The Battle of the Little Bighorn took place on a hot afternoon, the 25th of June, 1876.

There were close to 1800 Indian warriors—mostly Sioux and Cheyenne led by Sitting Bull and Crazy Horse—outnumbering the U.S. Army commanded by George Armstrong Custer nearly 3 to 1.

Additional troops led by Colonel John Gibbon were due to arrive in the area the next day, and Custer also expected General George Crook to be arriving soon with reinforcements, coming up from the south. What Custer did not know was that Crook had been defeated by the same warriors he was about to face the week before at the Battle of the Rosebud, 30 miles to the southeast.

Afraid that the Indians would scatter if he waited for Gibbon and Crook, Custer decided to attack.

Custer divided his column, sending Captain Frederick Benteen with a battalion of troops on a wide arc to the south to prevent the Indians from escaping. He then ordered Major Marcus Reno to attack the southern end of the village with his 175 troops.

Reno's charge was quickly repelled, sending his men retreating up into the bluffs overlooking the Little Bighorn River. With Reno pinned down, and Benteen miles away with the pack train of ammunition, Custer and his troops became cut off, allowing the Indian warriors to overrun them.

Custer's entire command of over 200 men was wiped out.

VIEW OF LITTLE BIGHORN FROM RENO HILL

LAST STAND HILL

WHAT'S THERE TODAY: Last Stand Hill sits reflectively overlooking the Montana landscape with markers to show where Custer and his soldiers fell. There are also markers to identify some of the Indians who died during the battle.

A short drive along a paved ridge leads to where Reno and his men were pinned down.

There is a cemetery just down from Last Stand Hill that holds the remains of soldiers from many of the nation's wars. Major Marcus Reno and Capt. William J. Fetterman (see page 44) are buried there.

The visitor's center at the battlefield includes artifacts, Custer memorabilia, and information on the battle. There is also an Indian memorial near Last Stand Hill.

ADDITIONAL INFORMATION: The battlefield is open every day (except New Years, Thanksgiving, and Christmas). Admission is charged per vehicle (more for larger vehicles), and a smaller fee for motorcycles and pedestrians. There is no charge for visiting the National Cemetery.

For more info call **406.638.3214**.

WEBSITE: www.nps.gov/libi/

Directions

From Sheridan take I-90 west for 76 miles. Follow the signs.

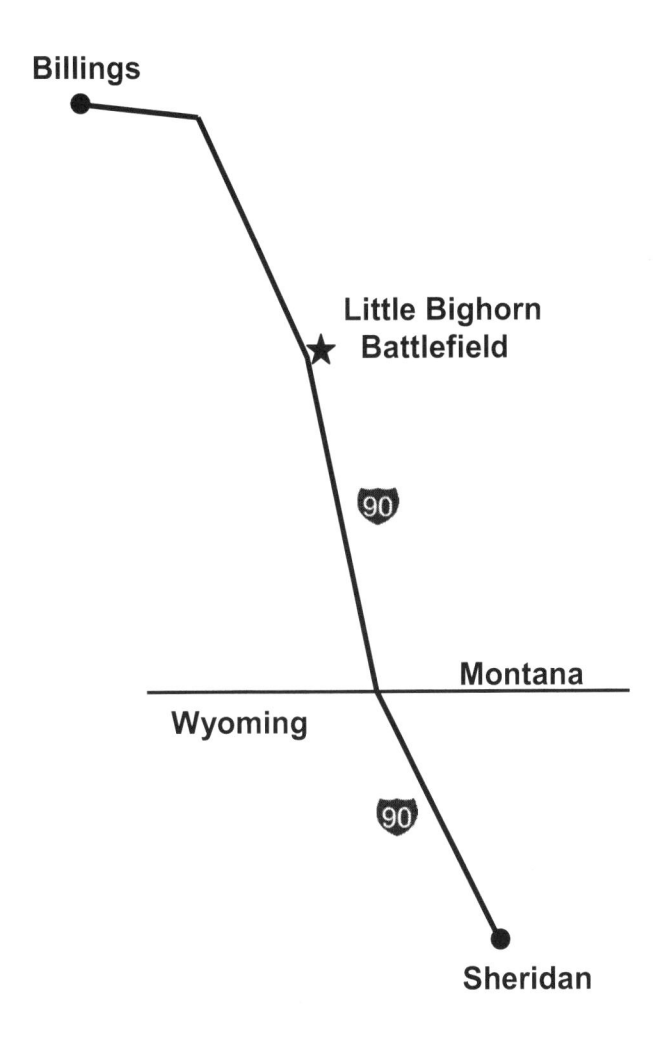

Billings

★ **Little Bighorn Battlefield**

(90)

Montana
Wyoming

(90)

Sheridan

22

~Devil's Tower~

History: It was designated the United States first national monument in 1906, although it is probably better known today from being featured in Steven Spielberg's movie *Close Encounters of the Third Kind*. The Lakota Indians call it Mato Tipila, meaning Bear Lodge. It is believed the name Devil's Tower came about in 1875, when on an expedition into the Black Hills led by Colonel Richard Dodge, an interpreter misinterpreted the name to mean Bad God's Tower, which was later shortened to Devil's Tower.

Some scientists believe the 867ft igneous rock tower is the remains of an ancient volcano. Others speculate that hot magma was pushed up from below the surface of the earth but without forming a crater. As the molten rock underneath cooled and the soft rock above wore away, the igneous rock below eventually become exposed.

While scientists debate its origin, many of the area's Indians use ancient myths to explain how Devil's Tower came to be. The most widely circulated involves two young girls who were chased by a bear while playing in the woods. When the girls jumped on top of a rock for safety, The Great Spirit, seeing the girls' predicament, caused the rock to grow to an immense size. The giant bear climbed up the side to pursue the girls but slipped down, its huge claws leaving gouges in the side of the rock that you see today.

Versions of this story are found among the Lakota, Blackfeet, Crow, Arapaho, and other Plains tribes. Many Indians still view Devil's Tower as a sacred site, traveling there for sun dances, vision quests, sweat lodge rituals, and to leave prayer bundles and offerings.

The columns of rock that make up Devil's Tower can be 4, 5, 6, or 7 sided. Some geologists believe the last column fell about 10,000 years ago.

The top of Devil's Tower is about the size of a football field. Its rocky on top and slightly domed in shape, with native grasses, cacti, and sagebrush.

WHAT'S THERE TODAY: Devil's Tower rises 1267 feet above the Belle Fourche River, which winds through the 1347 acre national park. There is a visitor's center, hiking trails, and camping facilities.

> **ADDITIONAL INFORMATION:** Hundreds of mountain climbers ascend Devil's Tower each year. There is a voluntary climbing closure each June out of respect for American Indians who hold sacred ceremonies throughout the month.
>
> Devil's Tower National Monument is open year round. However, the visitor's center is closed through the winter.
>
> For more info call **307.467.5283**.

WEBSITE: www.nps.gov/deto

Directions

I-90 East to Moorcroft, Wyoming (130 miles). From Moorcroft take Hwy 14 north to Hwy 24. Follow Hwy 24 north to Devil's Tower.

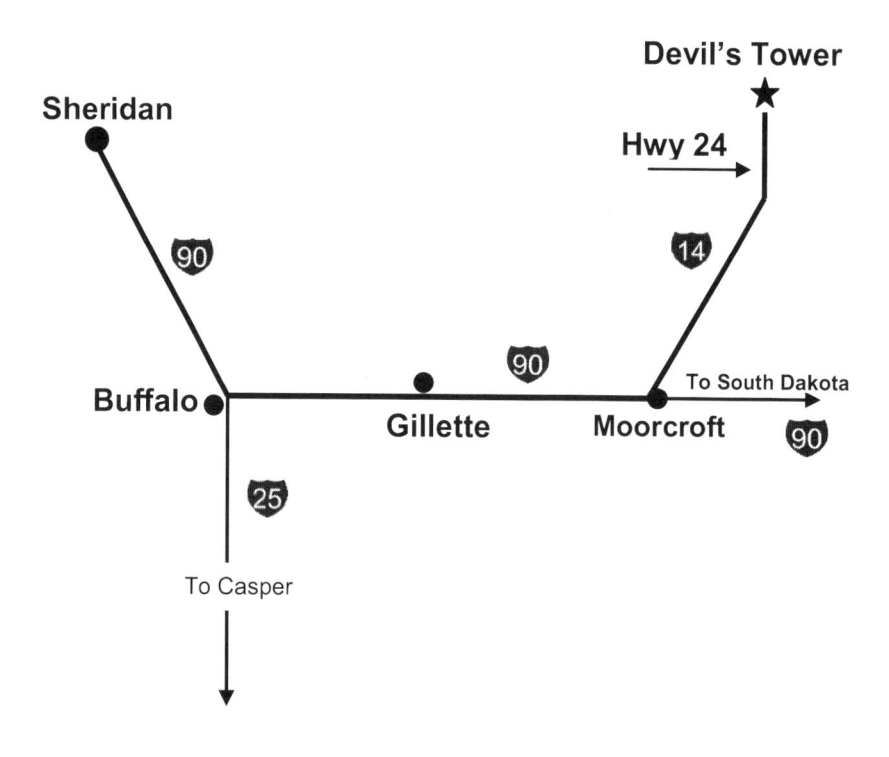

That's Here? Sheridan, WY

POMPEY'S PILLAR

Called Iishiia Anaache or "Place Where the Mountain Lion Dwells" by the Apsaalooka (Crow) people, Pompey's Pillar was a well-known landmark to the Plains Indians. It was here, at a strategic natural crossing of the Yellowstone, or Elk River as it was known to the Apsaalooka, that the Indian people met to trade and exchange information. They painted pictographs and etched petroglyphs onto the sheer cliffs of the feature. Apsaalooka legend reports that Pompey's Pillar was once attached to the sandstone bluffs on the north side of the river. At one point, however, the rock detached itself from the cliffs and rolled across the river to its present site.

Pompey's Pillar was also a significant landmark for Euro-American explorers, fur trappers, soldiers and immigrants. It was discovered by Canadian North West Company employee Francois Larocque in 1805. A little less than a year later, on July 25, 1806, it was visited by a 12 man detachment under the command of William Clark that included Sacajawea and her infant son. Clark carved his name and the date on the rock and named it in honor of Sacajawea's son. He was just one of hundreds of individuals who for generations have left their marks on the rock.

23

POMPEY'S PILLAR

HISTORY: Pompey's Pillar remains the only piece of physical evidence left behind by the Lewis and Clark expedition of 1804-1806. On July 25, 1806, William Clark carved his name on the sandstone butte in southeastern Montana, during his return trip from the Pacific Ocean.

Clark named the formation "Pompey's Tower" for Sacagawea's (the party's interpreter and Indian guide) son, Jean Baptiste Charbonneau, who Clark fondly called Pomp. Later, in the first edition of the published Lewis and Clark journals, the name was changed to Pompey's Pillar and the name stuck.

Plains Indians called the pillar "the place where the mountain lion lies." Some believe the name derives from a sandstone formation on the pillar that resembles a mountain lion's head or from live mountain lions being spotted in the area.

The first recorded observation of Captain Clark's signature on Pompey's Pillar was by James Stuart in 1863. Stuart was a Montana pioneer and leader of a gold prospecting party down the Yellowstone Valley.

George Armstrong Custer and the 7th Cavalry camped at the base of Pompey's Pillar in 1873, coming under fire by Sioux warriors led by Crazy Horse.

> . . . At 4PM [I] arrived at the remarkable rock situated in an extensive bottom. This rock I ascended and from its top had a most extensive view in every direction. This rock which I shall call Pompy's Tower is 200 feet high and 400 paces in secumpherance and only axcessible on one side which is from the N.E. the other parts of it being a perpendicular clift of lightish coloured gritty rock. The Indians have made 2 piles of stone on the top of this tower. The nativs have ingraved on the face of this rock the figures of animals &c. (Jones 2000, 185-186)
>
> William Clark
> July 25, 1806

CLARK'S SIGNATURE AT POMPEY'S PILLAR

WHAT'S THERE TODAY: Clark's original etching of his name and the year are still in their original spot, although they are now encased behind glass to protect it. A boardwalk leads you to the spot. There is also a replica of Captain Clark's canoes at the nearby interpretive center, as well as a terrific view from atop the pillar of the Yellowstone River.

> **ADDITIONAL INFORMATION:** The Pompey's Pillar Interpretive Center is adjacent to the formation. The center offers exhibits of the Lewis and Clark Expedition, as well as the history of Pompey's Pillar through the ages.
>
> "Clark Days" are held the last weekend in July each year, featuring living history demonstrations and interpretive activities.
>
> The Monument is usually open to vehicles from late April until late September. There is an entrance fee for each vehicle (except for commercial and group visits, which fees are based on vehicle capacity).
>
> During the winter months you can walk in to the site during daylight hours.
>
> For more info call **406-875-2400**.

WEBSITE: www.pompeyspillar.org

VIEW ATOP POMPEY'S PILLAR LOOKING NORTHEAST

Directions

I-90 West towards Billings, MT (122 miles). Merge onto I-94 East (Exit 456). Proceed about 22 miles to Exit 23 and follow the signs.

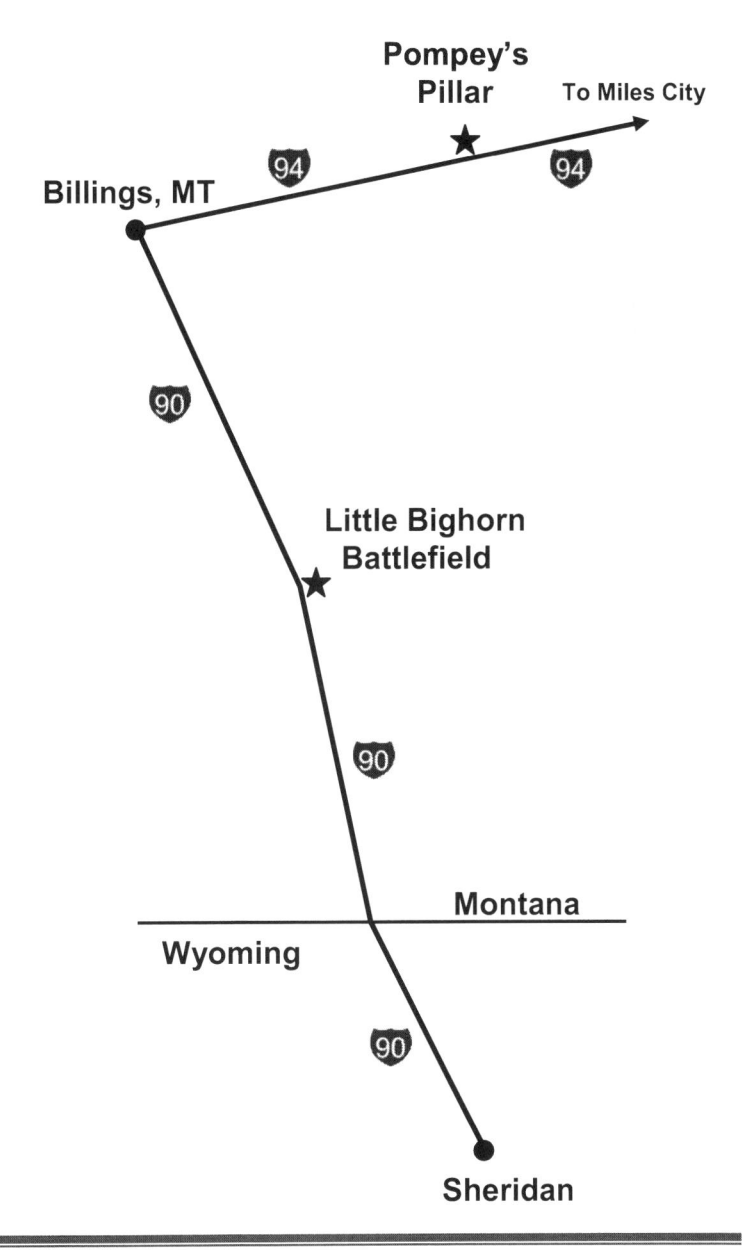

24

~Medicine Wheel~

History: Seventy-five feet in diameter with twenty-eight spokes, the Wyoming Medicine Wheel remains a mystery even today. It is supposed the wheel held some sort of spiritual significance, and the site is still thought of as sacred by many of today's Indian tribes.

There are many theories as to the original use of the Medicine Wheel. Some believe the wheel's 28 spokes represent the 28 days in a month, and 2 of the 6 cairns (a manmade pile of stones) mark the horizons of sunrise and sunset—the remaining 4 cairns marking the rising of the 3 brightest stars. Other archeologists counter that the Indians who built the Medicine Wheel had no use for an organized calendar because they were not farmers. Their theory is that the

Medicine Wheel carried religious significance and was used in religious ceremonies.

Crow tribal myth credits the wheel's creation to a boy named Burnt Face, who fell into a fire as a baby and was severely scarred. When Burnt Face became a teen, he went into the Bighorn Mountains seeking a vision quest. He fasted and built the Medicine Wheel. During his quest, Burnt Face helped drive away an animal that was attacking baby eaglets, so in return, an eagle carried him off and his face was made smooth.

Another Crow legend tells of Red Plume, a great Crow chief during the time of Lewis and Clark. Red Plume found great spiritual medicine at the Medicine Wheel. The legend tells that after four days without food or water, Red Plume was visited by little people who inhabited the passage to the wheel. They took him into the earth where they lived and told him that the red eagle feathers were his powerful medicine guide and protector. He was also told to always wear the small feather from the back of the eagle above its tail feathers—this is how Red Plume received his name. When he was about to die, Red Plume told his people his spirit would be found at the wheel and that they might communicate with him there.

The wheel, made of limestone slabs and boulders, is thought to have been created between 1200 and 1700 A.D. It was discovered by prospectors as late as 1885.

Chief Joseph of the Nez Perce tribe is said to have fasted at the Medicine Wheel, and Chief Washakie of the Shoshone tribe claimed to have obtained his medicine there.

Medicine Wheels have also been discovered in South Dakota, Montana, and in the Alberta and British Columbia area of Canada, as well as other areas of the world.

The Medicine Wheel of the Bighorn Mountains is one of the largest wheels found and is considered the most renowned.

WHAT'S THERE TODAY: The Medicine Wheel is pretty well intact considering its age. There are also other stone circles and tipi rings to see nearby.

> **ADDITIONAL INFORMATION:** Be on the lookout for ancient Indian artifacts on Medicine Mountain where the wheel is found. A protective fence surrounds the wheel and many Indians today place prayer cloths, along with other sacred symbolic items on the fence. Please respect these items and not disturb them. Also note: *it is illegal to take artifacts from the area.*
>
> The road that leads up to the Medicine Wheel from the interpretive site does not permit motorized vehicles, except for handicap accessibility. You will have to walk the last 1.5 miles, so bring water. Access is weather permitting—usually about June to October.

WEBSITE: www.medicinewheel.com

PRAYER CLOTHS LEFT AT MEDICINE WHEEL

DIRECTIONS

I-90 west to Hwy 14W at Ranchester. Take Hwy 14W into the Bighorn Mountains, veering onto Hwy 14A (about 30 miles from Dayton) which takes you to Lovell, WY. Follow the signs to the Medicine Wheel (about 26 miles).

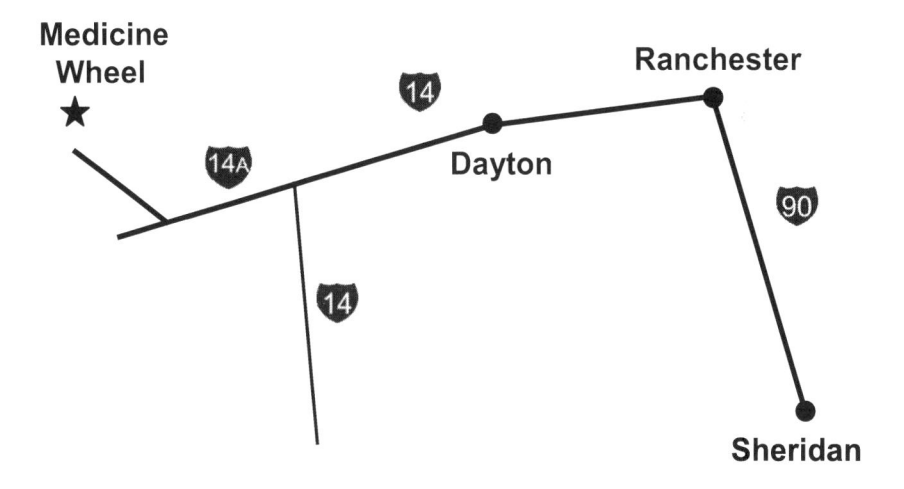

25

~Deer Medicine Rocks~

History: In early June of 1876, only weeks before the Battle of the Little Bighorn, Sitting Bull and the Lakota Sioux were camped on Rosebud Creek, just north of modern day Lame Deer, Montana.

There the Lakota held their annual Sun Dance, a religious ceremony where they prayed and sacrificed themselves to Wakan Tanka—the Great Mystery. After cutting 50 pieces of flesh from each of his arms, Sitting Bull then danced for hours gazing directly into the hot sun, before finally collapsing from fatigue and loss of blood. When he awoke he told of a great vision that he had received. The American soldiers, who were now pursuing them, would fall into their camp like grasshoppers, and the Lakota would enjoy a great victory over them. Three weeks later the vision was confirmed when soldiers at the Battle of the Little Bighorn were literally carried into the village atop their spooked horses.

Sitting Bull's vision was carved onto the sandstone rocks in the area, which had been a sacred place for Plains Indians for generations.

George Armstrong Custer also camped in this area with the 7th Cavalry a few weeks later, as he tracked Sitting Bull and Crazy Horse before the Battle of the Little Bighorn.

WHAT'S THERE TODAY: The Deer Medicine Rocks appear today as they did when Sitting Bull imprinted the story of his vision onto the rocks, although some of the carvings are fading. Crazy Horse also carved pictures into the sandstone, prophesying his death by getting stabbed in the back by a soldier. There are many other Indian carvings on the surrounding rocks, some dating back thousands of years.

> **ADDITIONAL INFORMATION:** The Deer Medicine Rocks are on private land, but they can be seen from Hwy 39, which actually runs over the old Sun Dance grounds. The town of Lame Deer is 7 miles to the south where the offices for the Cheyenne Nation are located. Cheyenne Chief Dull Knife is buried in the cemetery in Lame Deer.

AREA OF SITTING BULL'S SUN DANCE

DIRECTIONS

Take Decker Road (Hwy 338) north from Sheridan about 63 miles to Busby, MT. **Note: Wyoming Hwy 338 turns into Montana Hwy 314 at the Wyoming/Montana state border.** From Busby, proceed on US 212E 16 miles to Lame Deer, MT. Turn left onto Hwy 39 N for about 7 miles. Deer Medicine Rocks will be on your left (to the west).

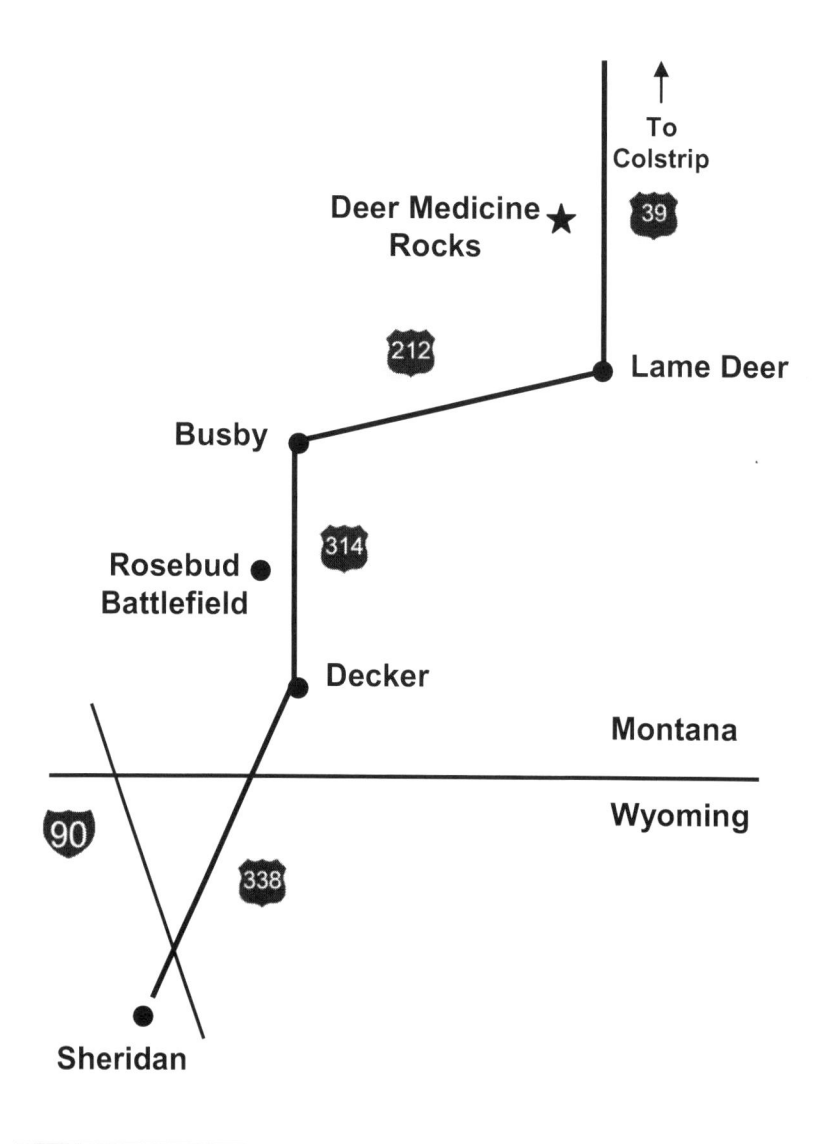

Historic Downtown

Sheridan

~Historic Downtown Sheridan~

Sheridan County Courthouse
224 South Main Street

Completed in 1905, it remains the Sheridan County Courthouse today. At one time the complex included the county jail and a sheriff's residence in the back.

Sheridan County Courthouse

Western Hotel Building
100 South Main

Today it is an apartment building. Built in the early 1900's with an impressive lobby, it was the starting point for the Sheridan Trolley that ran out to Fort Mackenzie and the coal mines north of town.

Kutcher Building
52 South Main

This northwest corner of Works and Main Street was the site of Sheridan's first blacksmith shop. Build in 1920 it is used as an office building today.

First National Bank
2 North Main

Sheridan's original cabin (the Mandel Cabin-see page 16) operated a bank here in 1890. It is still the current location of a local bank.

WYO Theater
42 North Main

Opened in 1923 and called the Lotus Theater, it became known as the WYO Theater in 1941. Renovated in 1989, it has been home to many leading shows and musical acts over the years.

Dr. Lever's residence

SHERIDAN'S ORIGINAL FIREHOUSE

ORIGINAL FIRE STATION
112 North Main

Now a bar, this building originally housed Sheridan's fire station and town hall. The arched windows that remain today are where the horses and wagons exited the fire house.

PALACE CAFE
138 North Main

Opened in 1910, the Palace Cafe is still in business today serving up breakfast and lunch. It is one of Sheridan's longest running businesses occupying its original location.

THE KENDRICK BUILDING
234 North Main

Home to one of the oldest J.C. Penny's department stores in the country. A livery stable was located here before John B. Kendrick constructed the building in 1906. Kendrick made the upstairs his office for many years.

Bucket of Blood Saloon
302 North Main

This northwest corner of Main & Alger was the location for the Bucket of Blood Saloon in the early 1890's. This was a part of Sheridan's "Red Light" district at that time, but by the late 90's the saloon had become a hotel. The building you see today was built in 1908.

Cady Opera House
302 North Main

Originally a 3 story building, the top floor which was the Cady Opera House burned in 1906 and was never rebuilt. Built in 1893, the building has been home to a grocery store, post office, and temporary courthouse. Today it is home to a restaurant and offices.

The Mint Bar
151 North Main Street

Opened for business in 1907 it continues to be a gathering spot for the "locals" of Sheridan. The style exhibited by the bar today dates back the late 1940's.

The Mint Bar

J.H. Conrad Store
1 South Main

It is the only false fronted building that remains from Sheridan's early years. Built in 1883 as Sheridan's first general store, it is also the oldest building in Historic Downtown Sheridan. Today it is home to a pharmacy.

Dr. E. E. Levers Residence
49 South Main

Used originally as a doctor's office and residence. It is the only house still residing in Sheridan's Historic Downtown. Today it is a lawyer's office and apartment.

Keenan Building
101 South Main

The Keenan building occupies the site of Sheridan's first hotel, The Grand Central. The current brick building was built in 1916 by Dick Keenan, then president of a nearby coal company. A realty office makes the building its home today, along with some rental apartments on the top floors.

Keenan Building

More to See

KENDRICK PARK
830 Beaver (Corner of Badger & Beaver)

If you want to see up close a real life buffalo or elk, Kendrick Park is the place. Both roam freely in the upper portion of the park, while the section below is reserved for playgrounds and picnic spots.

Kendrick Park at one time had a zoo, complete with wolves, monkeys, and an assortment of other animals. The family of John Kendrick, who built his mansion (see page 20), Trails Inn, on the bluffs above, donated the land back in 1936.

Today Kendrick Park is an appealing city park complete with hundred year old ponderosa pine trees, children's playgrounds, and Big Goose Creek, which runs through it on one side.

The two lion-dogs guarding Kendrick Park were once a part of the exterior decoration (used in the Chinese government's section) at the Panama Pacific International Exposition in San Francisco in 1915. A Sheridan butcher, who visited the Exposition, bought them and originally displayed them in front of his house on Loucks Street before they were moved to the park.

BUFFALO AT KENDRICK PARK

CIVIL WAR CANNON IN SHERIDAN CEMETERY

CIVIL WAR CANNONS
Sheridan Cemetery, 1000 Ash Ave

2 Civil War cannons are displayed in the center of Sheridan's cemetery. The cannons were used in the war and were made at a Boston foundry owned by the family of Paul Revere. The cannons were given to the city of Sheridan in 1912 by the John Schuler, Post No. 67, Grand Army of the Republic.

ELKS LODGE
45 W. Brundage (corner of Brooks & Brundage)

The Sheridan Elks Lodge was built in 1909 for around $50,000 (over $1 million in today's dollars). It was at the time one of the most modern lodges in the West. The Sheridan Elks Lodge #520 is the oldest B.P.O.E. lodge in the state of Wyoming. The Elks Lodge was for a time one of the bustling social centers for the community of Sheridan.

Sheridan Train Depot
201 E. 5th St (corner of 5th & Broadway)

Sheridan's original train depot is just west of the railroad tracks on 5th street, across from the Historic Sheridan Inn (see page 12). When the first passenger train arrived in Sheridan on November 18, 1892, the depot was located just south of its present location, where a local bar sits today. The brick building that is now a bar replaced the two-story wood depot in 1912. The original depot is part of the Sheridan Railroad Historic District on the National Register of Historic Places.

Original Sheridan Train Depot

CB&Q Locomotive
Rotary Park (across from Sheridan Inn)
Corner of 5th & Broadway

The locomotive on display ran on the Chicago, Burlington and Quincy line in the 1940's and 50's. It is a coal fired, combination freight and passenger locomotive built in 1940.

SHERIDAN AREA

MUSEUMS

~Sheridan Area Museums~

Sheridan County Museum
Sheridan, Wyoming
850 Sibley Circle (5th Street at I-90)
307.675.1150
www.sheridancountyhistory.org

Offers information and artifacts related to Sheridan's history, along with local Indian War history. There is an interactive exhibit on Crazy Horse and the Rosebud Battle, along with paintings and models.

Don King Museum
Sheridan, Wyoming
184 N. Main St
307.672.2702
www.kingropes.com

Home to over 500 saddles and assorted Cowboy memorabilia. The Old West museum also displays guns, wagons, and American Indian artifacts. Look close to find the buckskin pants worn by John Wayne in the movie *Red River*.

Bozeman Trail Museum
Big Horn, Wyoming
335 Johnson Street
307.674.1600

Housed in a refurbished blacksmith shop built in 1879, it is home to the Cloud Peak Boulder—a stone with names and dates carved by some of General George Crook's troops, just two days before the Battle of the Little Bighorn (see page 30). Also on display are artifacts of the area's local history.

Bradford Brinton Memorial & Museum
Big Horn, Wyoming
239 Brinton Road
307.672.3173
www.bbmandm.org

Collection includes original Western art by Charles Russell, Frederic Remington, and Hans Kleiber, along with American Indian artifacts, an original letter from Abraham Lincoln, and a George Washington document.

Jim Gatchell Museum
Buffalo, Wyoming
100 Fort Street
307.684.9331
www.jimgatchell.com

The museum features dioramas on local Indian War battle sites and the Johnson County War. There is an exhibit on the Bozeman Trial (see page 52) and a bugle reportedly found on the Fetterman Battlefield site (see page 44). Museum collection also contains artifacts from the Battle of the Little Bighorn.

Custer Battlefield Museum
Little Bighorn Battlefield
406.638.3214
www.www.nps.gov/libi/

The museum is home to battlefield artifacts and Custer memorabilia. Adjacent to the museum is the battlefield gift shop/bookstore with a terrific selection of books related to the Battle of the Little Bighorn (see page 94) and the Indian Wars.

Sheridan

Area Events

~Sheridan Area Historic Events~

Eaton's Ranch Horse Drive

Eaton's Ranch cowboys drive over 100 horses through the town of Sheridan. The horses are started east of Sheridan where they pasture for the winter, and are then herded down 5th Street past the Historic Sheridan Inn, across Main Street, and out to Eaton's Ranch. Date varies each year, but is usually in late May or early June.

www.eatonsranch.com
307.655.9285

Bozeman Trail Days

Living history presentations and special tours of Fort Phil Kearny (see page 40) and the Fetterman Battlefield (see page 44) highlight the weekend event. There are also period weapons demonstrations, along with camp and tipi exhibits. Typically held each year around the 2nd or 3rd weekend of June.

www.bozemantrail.org
307.684.7629

Sheridan WYO Rodeo

It's Sheridan, Wyoming's, premiere event. Held annually since 1931, people from all over the world converge on Sheridan for a week of events, centering around one of the top professional rodeos in the country. Events include 4 nights of PRCA rodeos, Indian pony relay races, parade, and street dances.

www.sheridanwyorodeo.com
307.672.9715

Fetterman Battle Anniversary

Held each year on the anniversary of the battle: December 21, 1866. Visitors begin with a short discussion at Fort Phil Kearny (see page 40), then travel by car 3 miles for a tour of the Fetterman Battlefield (see page 44). Rain, snow, or shine.

www.philkearny.vcn.com
307.684.7629

Custer Battle Reenactment

Custer buffs from all over the country pilgrimage to Hardin, Montana, each June to commemorate the Battle of the Little Bighorn (see page 94). The reenactment unfolds just outside of Hardin, about 15 miles north of the famous battlefield. The reenactment is a part of Little Bighorn Days (put on by the city of Hardin) that features a week of Custer themed events.

www.custerslaststand.org
406.665-1672

AUTHOR

David Wooten is also the author of two works of fiction: *Canaan Creek* and *Jerusalem Town*. He was born in Grants, New Mexico, and was raised in California. Dave moved to Sheridan, Wyoming, in 2005.